Adonis (the pen-name of Ali Ahmad Said) was born in Syria in 1930. He was exiled to Beirut in 1956 and later became a Lebanese citizen. The founder of the influential journal *Mawaqif,* a critic as well as a poet, he has exercised enormous influence on Arabic literature. He is the author of *Sufism and Surrealism*, also published by Saqi.

Mahmud Darwish was born in 1942 in al-Barweh, a village in Palestine. His first collection of poetry was published in 1960, and since then he has become perhaps the best-known Palestinian poet in the world.

Samih al-Qasim is a Palestinian born to a Druze family of Galilee in 1939. He grew up in Nazareth and has long been politically active in Israel, suffering imprisonment many times. A prolific writer, he had published six collections of poetry by the time he was thirty.

Adonis   Mahmud Darwish   Samih al-Qasim

VICTIMS OF A MAP

A Bilingual Anthology of Arabic Poetry

Translated from the Arabic by
Abdullah al-Udhari

SAQI

British Library Cataloguing-in-Publication Data
A catalogue record for this book is available from the British Library

ISBN 0 86356 524 7
EAN 9-780863-565243

First published in 1984 by Saqi Books
copyright © Abdullah al-Udhari, 1984 & 2005

This edition published 2005

SAQI
26 Westbourne Grove
London W2 5RH
www.saqibooks.com

Contents

Introduction

Ever since pre-Islamic days, poetry has been the mass art form of the Arab language. Through the centuries of classical Arab civilization in the Middle Ages, the long years of Arab decline, and into the decades of confrontation with European culture in the twentieth century, the poets have never lost their place of esteem in the minds of the people of the Arab world. In modern times, poets have had a greater impact on popular culture than novelists: there are more published poets than authors of literary prose in the Arab countries today, and public readings by poets consistently attract mass audiences, in settings ranging from rural villages to sprawling and sophisticated capital cities.

There can be little doubt that in this vast reservoir of talent, Mahmud Darwish, Samih al-Qasim, and Adonis are among the leading figures. Certainly their names would appear on nearly anyone's list of the best-known, most prolific, and most innovatory contemporary Arab poets. This book presents a selection of fifteen poems by each of them, with the original Arabic printed on the left-hand pages, the English translations on the right. All of them are newly translated for this volume. The first thirteen of Darwish's poems, written in November 1983 as the fighters of the Palestine Liberation Organization were preparing to leave Lebanon, are published here in Arabic for the first time in book form. The final poem of the collection, 'The Desert', by Adonis, appears here in Arabic for the first time ever. The poems of each contributor are introduced by brief biographical notes. From the information contained in these—and from the poems themselves, which speak more eloquently than any factual account of the lives of their authors—it will be clear how much these works express the fate not only of Arabs or Palestinians, but also of humanity itself trapped in a contemporary tragedy.

Modern Arab poetry has evolved against the background of the turmoil of the Arab world. The years since the end of the Second World War alone have seen five Arab-Israeli wars, major civil wars in Yemen and Lebanon, the repeated victimization of the Palestinian people, and a host of military coups in more than half a dozen countries. Through it all—in particular through the bitter disappointment with political leaders of various hues—the Arab people have looked to poets to express their aspirations. This is exemplified in the resistance poetry of the Palestinians Darwish and al-Qasim, whose poetic accomplishments have raised a local tragedy to the level of a universal one.

The evolution of poetry itself has also been marked by profound changes since the Second World War. The publication of two experimental poems by two Iraqi poets in 1947 marked the real inception of modern Arab poetry. In 1957 the Lebanese poet Yusuf al-Khal and Adonis launched their epoch-making poetry magazine *Shi'r*, whose contributions eventually led to the breakdown of classical Arab poetic conventions and redrew the map of Arab poetry. The role of Adonis in this literary upheaval has been central.

This collection is meant to provide English-speaking readers with a sense of the frontiers of Arab poetry today—and hopefully with some appreciation of the poetry in its own right as well.

I should like to express my indebtedness to George Wightman for his suggestions and encouragement.

Abdullah al-Udhari

The
Poems

Mahmud Darwish

Biographical Note

Mahmud Darwish was born in 1942 in the village of al-Barweh in Palestine. One night in 1948, the Israeli armed forces assaulted the village. The Darwish family fled through a forest, bullets winging overhead, and reached Lebanon, where they remained for more than a year, living on the meagre handouts of the United Nations. Finally, Darwish was led by his uncle back across the border to the village of Deir al-Asad, in Galilee. They could not return.to al-Barweh, for it had been obliterated by Israeli soldiers. 'All that had happened', Darwish told the Israeli Communist newspaper *Zo Hederekh* in an interview in 1969, 'was that the refugee had exchanged his old address for a new one. I had been a refugee in Lebanon, and now I was a refugee in my own country.'

The phrase was not simply metaphorical. Any Palestinian not accounted for in the first Israeli census was regarded by the new Israeli state as an 'infiltrator' and was therefore not entitled to an identity card. Darwish had been in Lebanon during the census and thus lived illegally in his own land. He recalled in the *Zo Hederekh* interview that both the Arab headmaster of his primary school and his parents used to hide him whenever police or other officials made an appearance. In the end, the family told the government that young Darwish had been with one of the Bedouin tribes of the North during the census. He was thus able to acquire an identity card.

Darwish became interested in poetry very early. He read much classical Arab literature when still at school, and in his first poetic attempts, he imitated pre-Islamic poetry. He was soon to find, however, that poetry could land him in serious trouble. He was asked by his headmaster to take part in a celebration, in Deir al-Asad, of the anniversary of the founding of the state of Israel. 'There', Darwish says, 'I stood before the microphone for the first time in my life and read a poem which was an outcry from an Arab boy to a Jewish boy. I don't remember the poem, but I remember the idea of it: you can play in the sun as you please, and have your toys, but I can't. You have a house, and I have none. You have celebrations, but I have none. Why can't we play together?'

The next day, Darwish was summoned by the military governor, who insulted and threatened him. Darwish left the office shaken: 'I wept bitterly because he concluded by saying, "If you go on writing such poetry, I'll stop your father working in the quarry." I couldn't understand why a poem could disturb the military governor. He was the first Jew I met and talked to. His behaviour upset me. If that was how the Jews were, why should I speak to a Jewish boy? The military governor became a symbol of evil who harmed relations between the two peoples.

'A few months later I was transferred to another school, where I was fortunate enough to meet a Jewish woman teacher. She was completely different from the military governor. She wasn't just a teacher, she was like a mother. It was she who saved me from the fire of distrust. She was a symbol of the good work a Jew does for his people. She taught me to understand the Old Testament as a literary work. She also taught me to appreciate the poetry of Bialik for its poetic verve rather than for its political message. She never tried to force on us the official syllabus, which was devised to distort and discredit our cultural heritage. She demolished the walls of distrust erected by the military governor.'

Until 1971, Darwish worked as a journalist in Haifa. In that year, he left Israel for Beirut, where he remained until 1982. He now lives in Paris and edits the magazine *Karmal*. He has published ten collections of poetry, and was awarded the Lotus Prize in 1969 and the Lenin Peace Prize in 1983. He is probably the best-known Palestinian poet in the world.

تضيقُ بنا الأرضُ

تضيقُ بنا الأرضُ ، تحشرُنا في الممر الأخير ، فنخلع أعضاءَنا كي نَمُر
تَعُضرُنا الأرضُ . يا ليتنا قَمحُها كي نموت ونحيا . ويا ليتها أُمَّنا
لترحَمَنَا أُمَّنَا . ليتنا صُورٌ للصخُور التي سوفَ يحملُها حُلمُنا
مَرايا . رأينا وجوه الذين سيقتلهُم في الدفاع الأخير عن الروح آخرُنا
بكينا على عيد أطفالِهم . ورأينا وجوه الذين سيرمونَ أطفالَنَا
من نوافذِ هذا الفضاءِ الأخير . مرايا سَيُلْصقها نجمُنا
الى أين نَذهبُ بعد الحدودِ الأخيرةِ أين تطيرُ العصافيرُ بعد السماءِ الأخيرة
أين تنامُ النباتاتُ بعد الهواءِ الأخير ؟ سَنكتبُ أسماءَنا بالبخارِ الملونِ بالقرمزي
سنقطعُ كَفَ النشيد لِيُكملَهُ لحمُنا
هنا سنموتُ . هنا في الممرِّ الأخيرِ . هنا أو هنا سوفَ يَغْرِسُ زيتونهُ .. دمُنا .

The Earth Is Closing on Us

The earth is closing on us, pushing us through the last passage, and
we tear off our limbs to pass through.
The earth is squeezing us. I wish we were its wheat so we could die
and live again. I wish the earth was our mother
So she'd be kind to us. I wish we were pictures on the rocks for our
dreams to carry
As mirrors. We saw the faces of those to be killed by the last of us in
the last defence of the soul.
We cried over their children's feast. We saw the faces of those who'll
throw our children
Out of the windows of this last space. Our star will hang up mirrors.
Where should we go after the last frontiers? Where should the birds
fly after the last sky?
Where should the plants sleep after the last breath of air? We will
write our names with scarlet steam.
We will cut off the hand of the song to be finished by our flesh.
We will die here, here in the last passage. Here and here our blood
will plant its olive tree.

عندما يذهب الشهداء الى النوم .

عندما يذهبُ الشهداءُ أصحو ، وأحرسُهُمْ من هواةِ الرِّثاءْ
أقولُ لهم : تُصبحونَ على وطنٍ ، من سحابٍ ومن شجرٍ ، من سرابٍ وماءٍ
أهنئهم بالسلامة من حادث المستحيلِ ، ومن قيمةِ المذبحِ الفائضة
وأسرقُ وقتاً لكي يَسرقوني من الوقتِ . هل كُلنا شهداءْ ؟
وأهمسُ : يا أصدقائي اتركوا حائطاً واحداً لحبالِ الغسيلِ ، اتركوا ليلةً للغناءْ
أعلّقُ اسماءَكُمْ أين شئتُمْ فناموا قليلا ، وناموا على سلم الكرمةِ الحامضةْ
لأحرسَ أحلامكمْ من خناجر حُراسكمْ وانقلابِ الكتابِ على الأنبياءْ
وكونوا نشيدَ الذي لا نشيدَ لهُ عندما تذهبونَ الى النوم هذا المساءْ .
أقولُ لكم : تُصبحونَ على وطنٍ ، حملوهُ على فرسٍ راكضةٍ
وأهمسُ : يا أصدقائي لن تصبحوا مثلَنا .. حبلَ مِشنقةٍ غَامضةْ !

When the Martyrs Go to Sleep

When the martyrs go to sleep I wake up to guard them against
professional mourners.
I say to them: I hope you wake in a country with clouds and trees,
mirage and water.
I congratulate them on their safety from the incredible event, from
the surplus-value of the slaughter.
I steal time so they can snatch me from time. Are we all martyrs?
I whisper: friends, leave one wall for the laundry line. Leave a night
for singing.
I will hang your names wherever you want, so sleep awhile, sleep on
the ladder of the sour vine tree
So I can guard your dreams against the daggers of your guards and
the plot of the Book against the prophets,
Be the song of those who have no songs when you go to sleep tonight.
I say to you: I hope you wake in a country and pack it on a galloping
mare.
I whisper: friends, you'll never be like us, the rope of an unknown
gallows!

نخاف على حلم

نخافُ على حلم : لا تُصدِّق كثيراً فراشاتِنا
وصَدِّق قرابيننا إن أردتَ ، وبوصلةَ الخيل صدقْ ، وحاجتنا للشَّمالْ
رفعنا اليك مناقيرَ أرواحِنا . أعطنا حبة القمح ِ يا حُلمَنا . هاتِها هاتِنا
رفعنا اليك الشواطىءَ منذ أتينا الى الأرض ِ من فكرةٍ أوْزِنا موجتـين على
صخرةٍ في الرِّمالْ
ولا شيءَ ، لا شيء . نطفُو على قدم ٍ من هواء .. هواء تكسرَ في ذاتِنا
ونعرفُ أنك تَرتدَ عنا ، وتبني سجوناً تُسَمَّى لنا جنةَ البرتقالْ

ونحلم .. يا حلماً نشتهيه ، ونسرق أيامنا من تُجَّلِّيهِ فيما مضى من خرافاتِنا
نخاف عليك ومنك نخاف . اتضحنا معاً ، لا تصدق إذن صبر زوجاتِنا
سينسجن ثوبين ، ثم يبعن عظام الحبيب ليبتعن كأس الحليب لاطفالنا .
نخاف على الحلم منه ومنا . ونحلم يا حلمنا . لا تصدق كثيراً فراشاتِنا !

We Fear for a Dream

We fear for a dream: don't believe our butterflies.
Believe our sacrifices if you like, believe the compass of a horse, our
  need for the north.
We have raised the beaks of our souls to you. Give us a grain of
  wheat, our dream. Give it, give it to us.
We have offered you the shores since our coming to the earth born of
  an idea or of the adultery of two waves on a rock in the sand.
Nothing. Nothing. We float on a foot of air. The air breaks up within
  ourselves.
We know you have abandoned us, built for us prisons and called them
  the paradise of oranges.
We go on dreaming. Oh, desired dream. We steal our days from those
  extolled by our myths.
We fear for you, we're afraid of you. We are exposed together, you
  shouldn't believe our wives' patience.
They will weave two dresses, then sell the bones of the loved ones to
  buy a glass of milk for our children.
We fear for a dream, from him, from ourselves. We go on dreaming,
  oh, dream of ours. Don't believe our butterflies!

يُحَقُّ لنا أن نحبَّ الخريفَ

ونحنُ يُحَقُّ لنا أن نُحبَّ نهاياتِ هذا الخريفِ ، وأن نسألَهُ :
أفي الحقلِ مُتسعٌ لخريفٍ جديدٍ ، ونحن نُمددُ أجسادَنا فيه فحما ؟
خريفٌ يُنَكِّسُ أوراقَه ذهباً ، ليتنا ورقُ التين ، يا ليتنا عشبةٌ مُهمَلهْ
لنشهدَ ما الفرقُ بين الفصولِ . ويا ليتنا لم نُوَدِّعْ جنوبَ العيونِ لنسألَ عما
تساءلَ آباؤُنا حين طاروُا على قمَّة الرمحِ . يرحمنا الشعرُ والبسمَلَةْ .
ونحن يحقُّ لنا ان نُجففَ ليلَ النساءِ الجميلاتِ ، أن نتحدثَ عما
يُقصرُ ليل غرييين ينتظرانِ وصولَ الشمالِ الى البوصلهْ
خريفٌ . ونحن يحَقُّ لنا أن نَشمَّ روائحَ هذا الخريفِ ، وأن نسألَ الليلَ حلماً
أيمرضُ حلمٌ كما يمرضُ الحالمونَ ؟ خريفٌ خريفٌ . أيولدُ شعبٌ على مقصلهْ ؟
يحق لنا أن نموتَ كما نشتهي أن نموتَ ، لتختبىء الأَرْضُ في سنبلهْ .

We Are Entitled to Love Autumn

We are entitled to love the end of this autumn and ask:
Is there room for another autumn in the field to rest our bodies like
  coal?
An autumn lowering its leaves like gold. I wish we were fig leaves
  I wish we were an abandoned plant
To witness the change of the seasons. I wish we didn't say goodbye
  to the south of the eye so as to ask what
Our fathers had asked when they flew on the tip of the spear. Poetry
  and God's name will be merciful to us.
We are entitled to dry the nights of lovely women, and talk
  about what
Shortens the night for two strangers waiting for the north to reach the
  compass.
An autumn. Indeed we are entitled to smell the scent of this autumn,
  to ask the night for a dream.
Does a dream fall sick like the dreamers? An autumn, an autumn.
  Can a people be born on the guillotine?
We are entitled to die the way we want to die. Let the land hide in an
  ear of wheat.

لديني .. لديني لأعرِفَ

لديني .. لديني لأعرفَ في أيِّ أرضٍ أموتُ وفي أي أرضٍ سأبعثُ حيّا
سلامٌ عليكِ وأنتِ تعِدّينَ نارَ الصباحِ ، سلام عليكِ .. سلام عليكِ .

أما آن لي ان أُقدِّمَ بعضَ الهدايا اليكِ : أما آن لي أن أعودَ اليكِ ؟
أما زال شَعرُك أطولَ من عمرنا ومن شجرِ الغيمِ وهو يَمُدُّ السماءَ اليكِ ليحيا ؟
لديني لأشربَ منكِ حليبَ البلادِ ، وأبقى صبيّاً على ساعديكِ وأبقى صبيا
الى أبد الآبدين . رأيتُ كثيراً يَ أمي رأيتُ . لديني لأبقى على راحتيكِ .
أما زلتِ حين تُحبيني تُنشدينَ وتبكين من أجل لا شيء . أمِّي ! أضعتُ يديا
على خصر إمرأةٍ من سَرابٍ . أُعَانِقُ رَمْلًا ، أُعَانِقُ ظِلًّا . فهل استطيع الرجوعَ
اليكِ / إليَّ ؟
لأُمّكِ أم ، لتين الحديقةِ غيمٌ . فلا تتركيني وحيداً شريداً ، أُريدُ يديكِ
لأحمِلَ قلبي . أحنُّ الى خُبزِ صَوْتِكِ أمي ! أحنُّ إلى كلِّ شيءٍ . أحنُّ إليَّ ..
أحن اليكِ .

Give Birth to Me Again That I May Know

Give birth to me again ... Give birth to me again that I may know
  in which land I will die, in which land I will come to life again.
Greetings to you as you light the morning fire, greetings to you,
  greetings to you.
Isn't it time for me to give you some presents, to return to you?
Is your hair still longer than our years, longer than the trees of clouds
  stretching the sky to you so they can live?
Give birth to me again so I can drink the country's milk from you and
  remain a little boy in your arms, remain a little boy
For ever. I have seen many things, mother, I have seen. Give birth to
  me again so you can hold me in your hands.
When you feel love for me, do you still sing and cry about nothing?
  Mother! I have lost my hands
On the waist of a woman of a mirage. I embrace sand, I embrace a
  shadow. Can I come back to you/to myself?
Your mother has a mother, the fig tree in the garden has clouds.
  Don't leave me alone, a fugitive. I want your hands
To carry my heart. I long for the bread of your voice, mother!
  I long for everything. I long for myself ... I long for you.

إذا كان لي أن أُعيد البِدَايَةِ

إذا كان لي أن أُعيد البداية ، أختارُ ما اخْتَرْتُ : وردَ السِّياج
أسافرُ ثانيةً في الدروبِ التي قد تُؤدّي وقد لا تُؤدي إلى قُرطُبَهْ .
أُعلّقُ ظِلي على صخرتين لتبني الطيورُ الشريدةُ عشاً على غصنِ ظِلِّي

وأكسر ظلي لأتبع رائحة اللوز وهي تطير على غيمة مُتْرَبَه
وأتعب عند السُّفوُح : تعالوا إلي اسمعوني . كلوا من رغيفي
اشربوا من نبيذي ، ولا تتركوني على شارع العمر وحدي كصفصافةٍ متعبه .
أحب البلاد التي لم يطأها نشيدُ الرَّحيلِ ولم تمتثِلْ لِدَمٍ وامرأةْ
أحب النساء اللواتي يُخَبِّئْنَ في الشَّهواتِ انتحارَ الخيُولِ على عتبه .
أعودُ ، اذا كان لي أن أعوُدَ ، إلى وردتي نفسِها والى خُطْوتي نفسِها
ولكنني لا أعودُ الى قُرْطُبَهْ .

If I Were to Start All Over Again

If I were to start all over again I'd choose what I had chosen: the roses
  on the fence.
I'd travel again on the road which may or may not lead to Cordova.
I'd hang my shadow on two rocks for the fugitive birds to build a
  nest on my shadow's branch,
I'd break my shadow to follow the scent of almonds as it flies on a
  dusty cloud,
And feel tired at the foot of the mountain: come and listen to me.
  Have some of my bread,
Drink from my wine and do not leave me on the road of years on my
  own like a tired willow tree.
I love the country that's never felt the tread of departure's song, nor
  bowed to blood or a woman.
I love the women who conceal in their desire the suicide of horses
  dying on the threshold.
I will return if I have to return to my roses, to my steps,
But I will never go back to Cordova.

أفي مِثْل هذا النشيد

أفي مِثل هذا النَّشِيدُ نوسدُ حلماً على صدر فارس

ونحملُ عنه القميصَ الأخير ، وشارةَ نصر ، ومفتاحَ آخِرَ باب

لنَدخلَ أولَ بحر ؟ سلامٌ عليك رفيقَ المكانِ الذي لا مكانَ لهُ

سلامٌ على قدميكَ / الرعاةُ سَيُنْسِونَ آثارَ عينيك فوقَ التُّراب

سلامٌ على ساعِديكَ / القَطاةُ ستعبُر ثانيةً من هنا

وسلامٌ على شفَتيكَ / الصلاةُ ستركَعُ في الحقلِ . ماذا نقولُ لجمرةِ عينيكَ .

ماذا يقول الغيابْ

لأمكَ ؟ في البئرِ نامَ ؟ وماذا يقول الغزاةُ ؟ انتصرناَ على غيمةِ الصوتِ في شهرِ

آبْ ؟

وماذا تقولُ الحياةُ لمحمودِ درويش ؟ عِشتَ .. عَشِقتَ .. عرفتَ ، وكل الذين

ستعشقُ ماتوا ؟

أفي مثل هذا النشيد نُوسدُ حلماً ونحملُ شارةَ نصرٍ ومفتاحَ آخِر باب

لنغلقَ هذا النشيدَ علينا ؟ ولكننا سوفَ نحيا .. لأنَّ الحياةَ حياةً .

Is It in Such a Song?

Is it in such a song we cushion the chest of a knight with a dream
Hold his last shirt, victory sign and the key to the last door
So we can plunge into the first sea? Greetings to you, friend of my
home, you who have no home.
Greetings to your feet/the shepherds will forget the traces of your
eyes on the soil.
Greetings to your arms/the sandgrouse will fly over here again.
Greetings to your lips/the prayer will bow in the field. What shall we
say to the embers in your eyes? What shall absence say
To your mother? He's asleep in the well? What shall the invaders say?
We have conquered the cloud of the voice in the month of August?
What does life say to Mahmud Darwish? You have lived, loved and
those you loved are dead?
Is it in such a song we cushion a dream, hold a victory sign and the
key to the last door
So as to shut this song from us? But we will live because life goes on.

لحن غجري

شارعٌ واضحٌ
وبنتٌ
خرجتْ تُشعلُ القمرْ
وبلادٌ بعيدةٌ
وبلادٌ بلا أثرْ .

حلمٌ مالحٌ
وصوتٌ
يَحفرُ الخصرَ في الحجرْ
إذهبي يا حبيبتي
فوقَ رمشي أو الوترْ .

قمرٌ جارحٌ
وصمتٌ
يكسرُ الريحَ والمطرْ
يجعلُ النهرَ إبرةً
في يدٍ تنسجُ الشجرْ .

A Gypsy Melody

A clear street
A girl
Goes out to light the moon,
And the country is far away,
A country without a trace.

A sour dream
A voice
Chisels a waist in a stone.
Go, my love,
On my eyelashes or the guitar strings.

A predatory moon
The silence
Breaks the wind and the rain,
Turns the river into a needle
In a hand weaving trees.

حائطٌ سابحٌ
وبيتُ
يختفي كلما ظهرْ
ربما يَقتلونَنا
أو يضيعونَ في الممرْ

زمن فاضح
وموتُ
يشتهينا إذا عبرْ
إنتهى الآن كل شيءٍ
واقتربنا من النَّهرْ
إنتهتْ رحلةُ الغجرْ
وتعبنا منَ السَّفرْ .

شارعٌ واضحٌ
وبنتُ
خرجتْ تُلصقُ الصورْ
فوقَ جدران جُثَّتي
وخيامي بعيدةٌ
وخيامٌ بلا أثرْ ...

A floating wall
A house
Disappears after it has been seen
Maybe they will kill us
Or lose their way in the alleyway.

A scandalous age
A death
Desires us while passing through.
Everything is finished now.
We're getting closer to the river
The gypsy's journey has come to an end.
We are tired of travelling.

A clear street
A girl
Goes out to stick pictures
On my body's wall,
And my tents are far away,
Tents without a trace.

نسافرُ كالنّاس

نسافرُ كالناسِ ، لكننا لا نعودُ الى أي شيء . كأنَّ السفرْ
طريقُ الغيومِ . دَفَنَّا أحبتنا في ظلام الغيومِ وبين جذوع الشجرْ
وقلنا لزوجاتنا : لِدْنَ منا مئاتِ السَنينَ لنكملَ هذا الرَحَيلْ
إلى ساعةٍ من بلادٍ ، ومترٍ من المستحيلْ .
نسافرُ في عربات المزاميرِ ، نـرقدُ في خيمـة الأنبياء ، ونخـرجُ من كلماتِ
الفجرْ .
نقيسُ الفضاءَ بمنقار هُدْهُدة أو نغني لِنُلهي المسافةَ عنا ، ونَغسلَ ضوءَ القمرْ .
طويلٌ طريقكَ فاحلم بسبعِ نساءٍ لتحملَ هذا الطريقَ الطويلَ
على كتفيكَ . وهزَّ لهن النخيلَ لِتَعْرفَ اسماءَهُن ومن أي أمٍ سيولدُ طفلُ الجليلْ
لنا بلدٌ من كلامٍ . تَكلم تكلمْ لأسندَ دربي على حجرٍ من حجرْ
لنا بلدٌ من كلامٍ . تكلم تكلمْ لنعرفَ حداً لهذا السفرْ !

We Travel Like Other People

We travel like other people, but we return to nowhere. As if travelling
Is the way of the clouds. We have buried our loved ones in the
   darkness of the clouds, between the roots of the trees.
And we said to our wives: go on giving birth to people like us
   for hundreds of years so we can complete this journey
To the hour of a country, to a metre of the impossible.
We travel in the carriages of the psalms, sleep in the tent of the
   prophets and come out of the speech of the gypsies.
We measure space with a hoopoe's beak or sing to while away the
   distance and cleanse the light of the moon.
Your path is long so dream of seven women to bear this long path
On your shoulders. Shake for them palm trees so as to know their
   names and who'll be the mother of the boy of Galilee.
We have a country of words. Speak speak so I can put my road on the
   stone of a stone.
We have a country of words. Speak speak so we may know the end of
   this travel.

نسيرُ الى بلدٍ

نسير الى بلدٍ ليسَ من لحمِنا . ليس من عظمِنا شجرُ الكَسْتَنَا
وليست حجارتهُ مَاعِزاً في نشيدِ الجبالِ .. وليست عيونُ الحصى سوسَنا
نسيرُ الى بلدٍ لا يُعَلِّق شمساً خصوصيةً فوقَنا .
تُصَفِّق من أجلِنا سيداتُ الأساطيرِ : بحرٌ علينا وبحرٌ لنا
اذا انقطَعَ القمحُ والماءُ عنكمْ ، كُلُوا حُبَّنا واشربوا دمعَنا .
مناديلُ سوداءُ للشعراءِ . وصفٌ تماثيلَ من مرمرٍ سوفَ يرفعُ أصواتِنا
وجرنٌ ليحمي أرواحَنا من غبارِ الزمان . وورد علينا ، وورد لنا
لكم مجدكُمْ ولنا مجدُنا . آه من بلدٍ لا نرى منهُ إلا الذي لا يُرى : سِرّنا
لنا المَجْدُ : عرشٌ على أرجلٍ قَطَّعَتْها الدروبُ التي أوصلتنا الى كل بيْبٍ سوى
بيتِنا !
على الروحِ أن تجدَ الروحَ في روحِها ، أو تموتَ هنا ..

We Go to a Country

We go to a country not of our flesh. The chestnut trees are not
   of our bones.
Its stones are not the goats in the mountain song, and the eyes
   of pebbles are not lilies.
We go to a country that does not hang a special sun over us.
The ladies of the myths clapped their hands for us. A sea for us
   and a sea against us.
If wheat and water are cut off from you, eat our love, drink our
   tears.
Black handkerchiefs for poets. A row of marble statues will
   raise our voices.
And a threshing floor to protect our souls from the dust of
   time. Roses for us and roses against us.
You have your glory, we have our glory. Ah, the country where
   we see only what is not seen: our secret.
The glory is ours. A throne on legs chapped by the roads that
   take us to every house except our house.
The soul should find its soul in its own soul or die here.

هنا نحنُ قرب هناكَ

هنا نحنُ قرب هناكَ ، ثلاثونَ باباً لخيمهْ .

هنا نحنُ بين الحصى والظلالِ مكان . مكانٌ لصوتٍ . مكانٌ لحريةٍ ، او مكانْ

لأي مكانٍ تدحرجَ عن فرسٍ ، أو تناثَرَ من جَرَسٍ أو أذانْ .

هنا نحن ، عما قليلٍ سنُثقبُ هذا الحصارَ ، وعما قليلٍ نحرّرُ غيمَه

ونرحلُ فينا . هنا نحنُ قرب هناكَ ثلاثوَن باباً لريح ، ثلاثونَ « كانْ »

نُعلّمُكم ان ترونا ، وأن تعرفونا ، وأن تسمعونا ، وأن تلمسوا دمنا في أمانْ

نُعلّمُكم سِلمَنا . قد نُحبُ وقد لا نحب طريقَ دمشقَ ومكةَ والقيروانْ .

هنا نحن فينا . سماءٌ لآبَ ، وبحر لمايو ، وحرية لحصانْ

ولا نطلبُ البحرَ إلا لنسحبَ منه دوائرَ زرقاءَ حول الدخانْ .

هنا نحن قرب هناكَ ، ثلاثونَ شكلاً ثلاثونَ ظلاً .. لنجمَهْ .

We Are Here Near There

We are here near there, the tent has thirty doors.
We are here a place between the pebbles and the shadows.
A place for a voice. A place for freedom, or a place
For any place fallen off a mare, or scattered by a bell or the
   muezzin's call.
We are here, and in a moment we'll explode this siege, and in a
   moment we'll free a cloud,
And travel within ourselves. We are here near there thirty
   doors for the wind, thirty "was",
Teaching you to see us, to know us, to listen to us, to feel our
   blood safely,
Teaching you our peace. We may love or may not love the road
   to Damascus, Mecca or Qairwan.
We are here within ourselves. A sky for the month of August,
   a sea for the month of May and freedom for a horse.
We seek the sea only to retrieve from it the blue rings round
   the smoke.
We are here near there thirty shapes, thirty shadows for a
   star.

مطارُ أثينا

مطارُ أثينا يُوَزِّعُنَا للمطاراتِ . قال المقاتلُ : أين أقاتلُ ؟ صاحت به حاملٌ أين أهديكَ طفلكَ ؟ قال الموظفُ : أين أوظفُ مالي ؟ فقال المثقفُ : مالي ومالكَ ؟ قـال رجالُ الجمـاركِ : من أين جئتمْ ؟ أجبنا : من البحـر . قال : الى أين تَمضونَ ؟ قلنا : الى البحرِ . قال : وأين عناوينُكم ؟ قالت امرأةٌ مِنْ جماعتنا : بُقجتي قريتي . في مطار أثينا انتظرنا سنيناً . تزوجَ شابٌ فتاةً ولم يجدا غرفةً للزواجِ السريعِ . تساءلَ : أين أَفُضُّ بكارتَها ؟ فضحكنا وقلنا لهُ : يا فَتَى ، لا مكان لهذا السؤالِ . وقالَ المُحلِّلُ فينا : يموتونَ من أجلِ ألا يموتوا . يموتونَ سهواً . وقالَ الأديبُ : مُخَيَّمُنَا ساقطٌ لَا محالةَ . ماذا يريدونَ منا ؟ وكانَ مطارُ أثينا يغير سكانَهُ كل يومٍ . ونحن بقينا مقاعدَ فوقَ المقاعدِ ننتظرُ البحرَ .. كم سنةً يا مطارَ أثينا !...

Athens Airport

Athens Airport boots us to other airports. A fighter said: "Where can I fight?" A pregnant woman blurted at him: "Where can we have our child?" An employee said: "Where can I invest my money?" An intellectual said: "Your money and mine?" The customs officers said: "Where do you come from?" We said: "From the sea." "Your destination?" "The sea." "Your address?" A woman in our group said: "My bundle is my village!" At Athens Airport we waited for years. A young couple got married and looked for a room in a hurry. The groom said: "Where can I deflower her?" We laughed and told him: "There's no room here for such a wish, young man." An analyst with us said: "They die so they may not die. They die overlooked." A writer said: "Our camp will inevitably fall. What do they want from us?" Athens Airport changes its people every day. But we have stayed put, seats upon seats, waiting for the sea. For how many years, Athens Airport?

يُحبونَني ميتاً

يحبونني ميتاً ليقولوا : لقد كان منّا ، وكانَ لنا .

سمعتُ الخطى ذاتِها . منذُ عشرينَ عاماً تدقُّ على حائطِ الليل . تأتي ولا تفتح البابَ . لكنها تَدخلُ الآنَ . يخرجُ منها الثلاثةُ : شاعرٌ ، قاتلٌ ، قارئٌ . ـ ألا تشربونَ نبيذاً ؟ سألتُ . سنشربُ ـ قالوا . متى تطلقون الرصاصَ عليَّ ؟ سألتُ . أجابوا : تَمَهَّل ! وصَفُّوا الكؤوسَ وراحوا يُغنون للشعب . قلتُ : متى تبدأون اغتيالي ؟ فقالوا : ابتدأنا .. لماذا بعثتَ الى الروح أحذيةً ؟ كي تسيرَ على الأرضِ ـ قلتُ . فقالوا : لماذا كتبتَ القصيدةَ بيضاءَ والأرضُ سوداء جِدّاً . أجبتُ : لأنَّ ثلاثينَ بحراً يَصُبُّ بقلبي . فقالوا : لماذا تحبُّ النبيذ الفرنسيَّ ؟ قلت : لأني جديرٌ بأجملَ إمرأةٍ ... ـ كيف تطلبُ موتك ؟ـ أزرقَ مثلَ نجومٍ تسيلُ من السقفِ ـ هل تطلبونَ المزيدَ من الخمر ؟ قالوا : سنشربُ . قلت : سأسألكُمْ أن تكونوا بطيئينَ ، أن تَقْتُلوني رُويداً رويداً لأكتبَ شعراً أخيراً لزوجةِ قلبي . ولكنهمْ يضحَكونَ ولا يسرقونَ من البيتِ غيرَ الكلامِ الذي سأقولُ لزوجةِ قلبي ...

They'd Love to See Me Dead

They'd love to see me dead so they can say: he was one of us, he belonged to us.

For twenty years I've heard those very steps banging on the night's wall. They came but did not open the door.

They have entered now. Then three of them went out: a poet, a killer and a reader. "Will you have a drink of wine?" I asked. "We'll have a drink", they said. "When will you shoot me?" I asked. They answered: "Take your time." They prepared the glasses and went on singing for the people. I said: "When will you start killing me?" They said: "We have started. Why did you send shoes to the soul?" "So it can walk on the land", I said. They said: "Why did you write a white poem when the land is jet black?" I answered: "Because thirty seas flow into my heart." They said: "Why do you like French wine?" I said: "Because I deserve the loveliest woman."

"How would you like your death?" "Blue like the stars pouring through the roof. Would you like some more wine?" They said: "We'll have some." I said: "I will ask you to do it slowly, to kill me slowly slowly so I can write the last poem for the wife of my heart." But they laughed and stole from the house only the words which I was going to say to the wife of my heart . . .

عازفُ الجيتارِ المتجول

كان رساماً ،
ولكنَّ الصورَ
عادةً ،
لا تفتح الأبواب
لا تكسرها ..
لا تردّ الحوتَ عن وجهِ القمر

(يا صديقي ، أيها الجيتارُ
خُذْيني ..
للشبابيكِ البعيدهْ) .

شاعراً كان ،
ولكنَّ القصيدهْ
يَبِستْ في الذاكرهْ
عندما شاهدَ يافا
فوقَ سطحِ الباخرَهْ .

(يا صديقي ، أيها الجيتارُ
خذني ..
للعيونِ العَسليَّهْ)

The Wandering Guitar Player

He was a painter
But pictures
Usually
Don't open doors
Nor break them
Nor turn the fish away from the face of the moon.

(Guitar friend,
Take me
To the distant windows.)

He was a poet
But the poem
Dried up in his memory
When he saw Jaffa
From a ship's deck.

(Guitar friend,
Take me
To the hazel eyes.)

كان جندياً ،
ولكنَّ شَظِيَّةً
طحنتْ ركبتهُ اليُسرى
فأعطوهُ هديَّةً :
رتبةً أخرى
وَرِجْلاً خَشَبِيَّةً !

(يا صديقي ، أيها الجيتارُ
خذني ...
للبلادِ النائِمهْ)

عازفُ الجيتار يأتي
في الليالي القادمهْ
عندما ينصرفُ الناسُ إلى جمعِ تواقيعِ الجنودِ

عازفُ الجيتار يأتي
من مكانٍ لا نراهُ
عندما يحتفلُ الناسُ بميلادِ الشُّهودِ
عازفُ الجيتار يأتي
عارياً ، أو بثيابٍ دَاخليَّةْ .

He was a soldier
But shrapnel
Crushed his left knee
And he was given
Another promotion
And a wooden leg!

(Guitar friend,
Take me
To the sleeping country.)

The guitar player is coming
Tomorrow night
When people go to collect soldiers' signatures.

The guitar player is coming
From a place we can't see.
The guitar player is coming
Naked or in his underwear
When people celebrate the day of witnesses.

عازفُ الجيتار يأتي
وأنا كدتُ أراهُ
وأشمُ الدمَ في أوتارِهِ
وأنا كِدت أراهُ
سائراً في كلِّ شارعْ

كدت أن أسمعهُ
صارخاً ملءَ الزوابعْ
حَدِّقوا :
تلكَ رجلٌ خشبيَّهْ
واسمعوا :
تلك موسيقى اللحومِ البَشَريَّهْ .

The guitar player is coming.
I can almost see him
And smell blood in his strings.
I can almost see him
Walking through every street.
I can almost hear him
Roaring:
"Have a good look,
      This is a wooden leg.
Listen,
      This is the music of human flesh."

مَطَرٌ ناعِمٌ في خريفٍ بعيدٍ

مطرٌ ناعِمٌ في خريفٍ بعيدْ
والعصافيرُ زرقاءُ .. زرقاءُ
والأرضُ عيدْ .
لا تقولي أنا غيمةٌ في المطارْ
فأنا لا أُريدْ
من بلادي التي سقطَتْ من زجاجِ القطارْ
غيرَ منديلِ أمي
وأسبابَ مَوْتٍ جديدْ .

مطرٌ ناعِمٌ في خريفٍ غَريبْ
والشبابيك بيضاءُ .. بيضاءُ
والشمسُ بيّارة في المغيبْ
وأنا برتقالٌ سليبْ ،
فلماذا تَفِرِّينَ من جسدي
وأنا لا أريدْ
من بلادِ السكاكين والعنادليبْ
غيرَ منديلِ أمِّي
وأسبابَ موتٍ جديدْ .

A Gentle Rain in a Distant Autumn

A gentle rain in a distant autumn
And the birds are blue, are blue,
And the earth is a feast.
Don't say I wish I was a cloud over an airport.
All I want
From my country which fell out of the window of a train
Is my mother's handkerchief
And reasons for a new death.

A gentle rain in a strange autumn
And the windows are white, are white,
And the sun is a citrus grove at dusk,
And I, a stolen orange.
Why are you running away from my body
When all I want
From the country of daggers and nightingales
Is my mother's handkerchief
And reasons for a new death.

مطرٌ ناعمٌ في خريفٍ حزين
والمواعيدُ خضراءُ .. خضراءْ
والشمسُ طينْ
لا تقولي رأيناكَ في مصرعِ الياسمينْ
آهِ ، بائعةَ الموتِ والاسبرينْ
كان وجهي مساءْ
وموتي جنينْ .
وأنا لا أُريدْ
من بلادي التي نسيتْ لَهجةَ الغَائِبينْ
غَيْرَ منديل أمي
وأسبابَ موتٍ جديدْ .

مطرٌ ناعمٌ في خريفٍ بعيدْ
والعصافيرُ زرقاءُ .. زرقاءُ
والأرضُ عيدْ .
والعصافيرُ طارتْ إلى زمنٍ لا يعودْ
وتريدين أن تعرفي في وطني ؟
والذي بيننا ؟
ـ وطني لذةٌ في القيودْ
ـ قُبلتي أُرسلتْ في البريدْ
وأنا لا أُريدْ
من بلادي التي ذبحتْني
غيرَ منديلِ أمي
وأسبابَ موتٍ جديدْ ..

A gentle rain in a sad autumn
And the promises are green, are green,
And the sun is of mud.
Don't say: we saw you in the killing of jasmine.
Ah, seller of aspirin and death,
My face was like the evening
My death a foetus.
All I want
From my country that's forgotten the speech of the distant
  ones
Is my mother's handkerchief
And reasons for a new death.

A gentle rain in a distant autumn
And the birds are blue, are blue,
And the earth is a feast.
The birds have flown to a time which will not return.
You'd like to know my country?
And what's between us?
My country is the joy of being in chains,
A kiss sent in the post.
All I want
From the country which slaughtered me
Is my mother's handkerchief
And reasons for a new death.

Samih al-Qasim

Biographical Note

Samih al-Qasim is a Palestinian from a Druze family of Rama, a village in
Galilee. He was born in Zarqa, Jordan, in 1939, when his father was
serving in the Arab Legion of King Abdullah, grandfather of Jordan's
King Hussein. He attended primary school in Rama, and later graduated
from a secondary school in Nazareth. In his *About Principles and Art*
(Beirut 1970), al-Qasim recalled the trauma of the 1948 war: 'While I was
still at primary school, the 1948 Palestinian tragedy occurred. I regard
that date as the date of my birth, because the first images I can remember
are of the 1948 events. My thoughts and images spring from the number
48.'

In the same volume he observed that the 'only way I can assert my
identity is by writing poetry'. And he has indeed been prolific. By the age
of thirty, he had published six collections of poems. As of 1984, he was
the author of twenty-four volumes of poetry, and he has also contributed
to the journals *al-Ittihad* and *al-Jadid*, among others. He regularly gives
readings of his poetry to large audiences in the Arab villages of Galilee,
and has been active not only as a poet, but also as a journalist.

He has been imprisoned many times for his political activities, which
involved defending the right of his people, and has suffered house arrest
as well. Nevertheless, he has remained in Israel, refusing either to leave
the country or to make his peace with the state authorities. In an inter-
view published in the journal *Index* in December 1983, he explained why:

'You know that part of Brutus's speech in which he says: "If then that
friend demand why Brutus rose against Caesar, this is my answer: not
that I love Caesar less, but that I love Rome more."

'I have chosen to remain in my own country not because I love myself
less, but because I love my homeland more.

'Once I was asked by my friend the Iraqi poet Buland al-Haidari if I had visited Baghdad. And I said simply that I haven't visited Baghdad or any Arab city. But I follow everything that goes on in those cities from my great prison. And I believe that if I was taken to any place in Damascus or Baghdad or Rabat, I have the feeling that I could walk through the streets as if I had been born and lived there for centuries. I feel there is no spiritual difference between Baghdad or Tunis or Jerusalem. I feel that all those countries belong to me. They are my homeland.'

Samih al-Qasim works as a journalist in Haifa, where he runs the Arabesque Press and the Folk Arts Centre.

الشفة المقصوصة

كان في وِدِّي ان أُسمِعكم
قصة عن عندليب مَيت
كان في وِدِّي أن أُسْمِعَكم
قصة ..
لو لَمْ يَقُصُّوا شَفَتي !

Slit Lips

I would have liked to tell you
The story of a nightingale that died.
I would have liked to tell you
The story...
    Had they not slit my lips.

أبناء الحَرْب

في ليلة الزِّفاف
سَاقُوه للحرب ،

ومرَّت .. خَمسةُ عِجَاف

ويوم أن عاد على حَمَّالةٍ حمراءْ
لَاقاهُ في الميناءْ
أبناؤُه الثَلَاثَةْ !

Sons of War

On his wedding night
They took him to war.

Five years of hardship.

One day he returned
On a red stretcher
And his three sons
Met him at the port.

اعتراف في عز الظهيرة

أنا غرستُ الشَّجرهْ
أنا احتقرتُ الثَمرهَ
أنا احتطبتُ جِذعَها
أنا صنعتُ العُودْ
أَنَا عزفتُ اللَّحن

أنا كسرتُ العودْ
أنا افتقدْتُ الثَّمَرَهْ
أنا افتقدتُ اللَّحن
أنا .. بكيتُ الشجرَهْ

Confession at Midday

I planted a tree
I scorned the fruit
I used its trunk as firewood
I made a lute
And played a tune

I smashed the lute
Lost the fruit
Lost the tune
I wept over the tree

تذاكر سفر

وعندما أُقْتَل في يوم ٍ من الأيام ْ
سَيَعِثرُ القاتلُ في جيبي
على تذاكرِ السَّفرْ
واحدة إلى السَّلامْ
واحدة إلى الحقولِ والمَطَرْ
واحدةٌ
الى ضمائر البشرْ
(أرجوكَ ألاَّ تُهْمِل التذاكِرْ
يا قَاتلي العزيزْ
أرجوكَ أن تُسافرْ ..)

Travel Tickets

On the day you kill me
You'll find in my pocket
Travel tickets
To peace,
To the fields and the rain,
To people's conscience.
Don't waste the tickets.

الخفافيش

الخفافيشُ على نافِذتي ،
تَمَصُّ صَوتي
الخفافيش على مدخل بيتي
والخفافيش وَراء الصُّحُف ،
في بعض الزَّوايَا
تَتَقصَّى خَطَواتي
والتفاتي

والخفافيشُ على المقعدِ ،
في الشارِع خلفي ..
وعلى واجهةِ الكتبِ وسيقان الصَّبايا ،
كيف دارت نظراتي !
... ...
الخفافيشُ على شُرْفة جاري
والخفافيش جهاز ما ، خَبِيءٌ في جدار
والخفافيش على وشك انتحَار
... ...
انني أحفرُ دَرْباً للنهَار !

Bats

Bats on the window
Suck my voice
Bats at the front of my house
Bats amongst the papers
Bats trail my steps
In corners
Wherever I turn
Bats on the chair
In the street behind me
On the books, up girls' legs
Where I can turn my gaze!
. . . .
Bats on my neighbour's balcony
Bats: some kind of apparatus
Concealed in the walls
Bats just about to kill themselves
. . . .
I am burrowing a passage to daylight!

التخلي

رأيتهُا ،
رأيتها .. في ساحة المدينَهْ
رأيتها نازفةً .. في سَاحةِ المدينَهْ
رأيتها مائلةً .. في ساحَةِ المدينَهْ
رأيتها مقتولَةً .. في سَاحَة المدينهْ
رأيتها .. رأيتها ..
وحين صاح :
من وَليُّ أمْرِها ؟
أنكَرْتها
أنكرتها في ساحةِ المدينهْ
أنْكَرْتها .. نَازِفَةً في ساحةِ المدينهْ
أنكرتها .. مائلة .. في ساحة المدينهْ
أنكرتها مقتولة .. في ساحة المدينهْ
أنكرتها ..

Abandoning

I saw her
I saw her in the square
I saw her bleeding in the square
I saw her staggering in the square
I saw her being killed in the square
I saw her . . . I saw her . . .
And when he shouted
Who is her guardian?
I denied knowing her
I left her in the square
I left her bleeding in the square
I left her staggering in the square
I left her dying in the square
I left her . . .

قصة مدينة

كانت هناك مدينةٌ زرقاءْ
تحلمُ بالأجانبْ
يتسكعونْ وينْفِقونْ
من الصباحْ .. الى الصباحْ
صارتْ هناك مدينةٌ سوداءْ
تحتقِرُ الأجانبْ
الدائرينْ على مقاهيها
بفوهاتِ السلاحْ ..

The Story of a City

A blue city
Dreamt of tourists
Shopping day after day.

A dark city
Hates tourists
Scanning cafes with rifles.

حوارية السُّنْبُلَةِ وَشَوكَةِ القُنْدُول

(المشهَدُ : حقلٌ على الشاطىءِ الشرقي للبحر المتوسط)

السُّنْبُلَة :	لا تقتُليني قبلَ ميعادي مع الموتِ الحياه
شوكة القندول :	القَتْل بالمجانِ مهنتي الوحيدَه
السنبلة :	لكن زهرتك الجميلَهْ
	عَسَلٌ ...
شوكة القندول :	وشهوتي العَنيدَه
	دَرْب .. ومَوْتُك مُنْتَهاهْ
السنبلة :	عيشي ومُوتي كيفَ شِئْت
	ما بين زهرتكِ الحزينه
	وظلام شهوتك اللَّعينَه
	عيشي وموتي .. واتْرُكيني
شوكة القندول :	قدر علينا .. أن تَعيشي كَيْ أموت
	أو أن تموتي كي أعيشْ
السنبلة :	في الحقل مُتَسَع لنا

Conversation Between an Ear of Corn and a Jerusalem Rose Thorn

*(Scene: a Field on the Eastern Shore
of the Mediterranean)*

Ear of Corn:

> Don't kill me before my time is up

Jerusalem Rose Thorn:

> To kill for nothing is my only profession

EC:

> But your lovely flower
> Is honey . . .

JRT:

> My unchecked desire
> Is a road . . . its end is your death

EC:

> Live and die as you wish
> With your sad flowers
> And the gloom of your cursed desire
> Live and die . . . but spare me

JRT:

> It's our fate . . . I die so you may live
> Or you die so I may live

EC:

> There's enough room for both of us in the field

شوكة القندول :   .. قَدر علينا
يا جارتي قَدر علينا

(تدخلُ النارُ وينهضُ الرعبُ)

السنبلة وشوكة القندول :
لا تَقْتُلينَا
يا نار ، نحن صغيرتانِ وحلوتانِ مَعاً رَبينا
لا تقتلينا
لا تقـ ...
(يبقى الرمادُ ، وسنبلة وشوكة قندولٍ على الأُفق)

JRT: It's our fate neighbour
            It's our fate
                (Enters Fire and Fear jumps up)
EC & JRT: Don't kill us fire
            We are young and pretty and we grew up together
            Don't kill us
            Don't ki . . .
                (Ashes, EC & JRT on the horizon)

يوم كنت سلعة

قتلوني مَرَّة
وانتحَلوا وجهي مِرَاراً

How I Became an Article

They killed me once
Then wore my face many times

قصة رجل غامض

في آخر الطريق كان واقفاً ، في آخر الطريقْ
كَشبَح الفَزَّاعة المنصوبِ في الكُرُومْ
في آخِر الطريقْ
كالرجل المرسوم فوق شارَةِ المُرُورْ
في آخِر الطريقْ
وفوق مَنْكَبيْهِ كان معطف عتيقْ
« الرجل الغامض » كان اسمُه
وكانتِ المنازلُ البيْضاءْ
تُغلقُ دونَ وَجْهِهِ أبوابَها
وشجراتُ الياسمينَ وَحْدها
كانت تحبُّ وجهه المصقول بالحب والبَغْضاءْ
... ...
« الرجلُ الغامضُ » كان إسْمه
وكانتِ البلادْ
ترزح تحت الحزنِ والجَرادْ
وصار ياما صارَ في يومٍ من الأيامْ
إن سار للأَمامْ

وجَلْجَلَتْ صرختهُ في ساحةِ المنازلِ البيضَاءْ
وازدحمَ الشيوخُ والأطفالُ وَالرَّجَالُ والنساءْ
في ساحةِ المنازلِ البيضَاءْ

The Story of the Unknown Man

At the end of the road,
At the end of the road he stood
Like a scarecrow in a vineyard.
At the end of the road he stood
Like the man in the green traffic light.
At the end of the road he stood
Wearing an old coat:
His name was the "Unknown man",
The white houses
Slammed their doors on him,
Only jasmine plants
Loved his face with its shadows of love and hate.

His name was the "Unknown man".
The country was
Under the weight of locusts and grief.
One day
His voice rang in the square of white houses.
Men, women and children
Thronged to the square of white houses

وأبصروهُ يَضْرُمُ النِّيرانْ
في المعطف العَتيقْ
(وكان فوقَ مَنكبَيهِ المعطف العَتيقْ)
وصَارَ يَامَا صارْ

أن السماءَ اَخْتَنَقَتْ بغيمةٍ خضراءْ
وغيمةٍ بيضاءْ
وغيمةٍ سوداءْ
وغيمةٍ حمراءْ
وغيمةٍ غامضة بدونِ لَونْ

وصَار يَاما صارْ
أن أَبْرقتْ وأرْعدتْ
وٱنْهَمَرَتْ أمطارْ
وانهمرت أمطار
الرجل الغامضُ كان اسمهُ
وشجرات الياسمين وحدَها
كانت تحب وجههُ المصقولَ بالحب والبغضَاءْ
وأصبحت تُحبُّهُ المنازلُ البيضاءْ

And saw him burning
His old coat.
(And he had an old coat.)

The sky swelled with a green cloud,
With a white cloud,
With a black cloud,
With a red cloud,
With a strange colourless cloud.

And on that day
The sky flashed and thundered,
The rain poured down
The rain poured down.
His name was the "Unknown man",
Only jasmine plants
Loved his face with its shadows of love and hate
And the white houses began to love him.

خاتمةُ النقَاشِ مع سَجَّانٍ

من كُوةٍ زنزانَتي الصغرى
أبصرُ أشجاراً تَبْسَمُ لي
وسطوحاً يملُأها أهلي
ونوافذ تبكي وتصلّي
من أجلي
من كوةِ زنزانَتي الصغرى
أبصرُ زنزانتكَ الكبرى

End of a Discussion With a Jailer

From the window of my small cell
I can see trees smiling at me,
Roofs filled with my people,
Windows weeping and praying for me.
From the window of my small cell
I can see your large cell.

أبدية

تتبدلُ الأوراقُ من آنٍ لِآنْ
لكن جذْعَ السِّنْدِيَانْ ..

Eternity

Leaves fall from time to time
But the trunk of the oak tree

وصية رجل يحتضر في الغربة

أو قِدُوا النارَ حتى أرى في مَرايا في اللَّهَبْ
ساحة الدار والقنطرَهْ
ومروجَ الذهَبْ
أو قدوا لي النارْ حتى أرى أدْمُعي
ليلة المجزرَهْ
وأرى أختكم جُثة
قلبها طائر مزَّقته اللغاتُ الهجينَهْ
والرياحُ الهجينَهْ
أو قِدُوا النارَ حتى أرى أختكُمْ
جُثَّةً .. وأرَى الياسمينَهْ
كفناً ..
والقَمَر ..
مِبْخَرَهْ
ليلةَ المجزَرَهْ
أو قِدوا النار حتى أرَى أنني أحتضِرْ
كل مِيراثِكُمْ حَسْرَتي
حَسْرَتي قبلَ أن تُصبح الياسمينهْ
شاهِداً ..
والقمرْ ..
شاهداً
أوقدوا النار حتى تَرُوا
أوقِدوا النـ ...

The Will of a Man Dying in Exile

Light the fire so I can see in the mirror of the flames
The courtyard, the bridge
And the golden meadows.
Light the fire so I can see my tears
On the night of the massacre,
So I can see your sister's corpse
Whose heart is a bird ripped up by foreign tongues,
By foreign winds.
Light the fire so I can see your sister's corpse,
So I can see jasmine
As a shroud,
The moon
As an incense burner
On the night of the massacre.
Light the fire so I can see myself dying.
My suffering is your only inheritance,
My suffering before the jasmine turns
Into a witness,
The moon
Into a witness.
Light the fire so I can see
Light the fi . . .

الدَّوْرَةُ البَاهِضَةُ

سَأَلتني ابنتي التي لم تولد بعد والتي اسمها (هَاجِرُ) : لماذا تدور الأرضُ يا أبي ؟
ـ استيقظ سبحانه ذات فَجْر
فجاءَهُ الملاكُ جبْرَائيلُ بقهوةِ الصَّباحِ
(ملعقةٌ واحدة من فضلك)
حرَّكَ سبحانَه السكَّر بملعقته الذَّهبيَّة
في دوائرَ مُفْرغةٍ رتِيبَةٍ
دوائر رتيبة
مُفْرغة ، دوائر رتيبة
ومنذ ذلك الوقت يا ابنتي
تدور الأرض دوراتها الباهظة ..

The Boring Orbit

My daughter who's not yet born and whose name is *Hagar*
asked me: "Daddy, why does the earth go round?"
"Early one morning God woke up
And the angel Gabriel brought Him his morning coffee.
'One sugar, please.'
God stirred the sugar with his gold spoon
In dull, empty circles,
Dull circles,
Dull, empty circles.
And since that time, my child,
The earth's been rotating in its boring orbit."

ساعةُ الحَائِط

مدينتي انهارتْ ،
وظلت ساعة الحائطْ
وحَيِّنَا انهار ،
وظلت ساعة الحائط
والشَّارعُ انْهَارَ ،
وظلتْ ساعةْ الحائطْ
والساحة انهارتْ
وظلت ساعةُ الحائطْ
ومنزلي انهار ،
وظلت ساعة الحائط
والحائط انهار ،
وظلتْ ..
ساعةُ الحَائِطْ ..

The Clock on the Wall

My city collapsed
The clock was still on the wall
Our neighbourhood collapsed
The clock was still on the wall
The street collapsed
The clock was still on the wall
The square collapsed
The clock was still on the wall
The house collapsed
The clock was still on the wall
The wall collapsed
The clock
Ticked on

Adonis

Biographical Note

Adonis (Ali Ahmad Said) was born in the village of Qassabin, Syria, in 1930.

> He came at the end of the night, at the season
> of old age.
> He never slept in a bed of myths
> He didn't live his childhood.

When he was fourteen years old, Adonis read a poem he had written before the newly elected president, then making a cross-country tour of Syria, which had just gained its independence. The poem urged the president and the people to cooperate in the building of the future of their country. The president was so impressed by the poem that he gave Adonis a grant to continue his studies. He went to school in Latakia. It was during this period that Adonis came under the influence of the literary and socio-political writings of Anton Sa'ada, which left an indelible mark not only on the work of Adonis, but also on modern Arab poetry.

In 1950 he enrolled at Damascus University and read literature and philosophy. He began writing and publishing poems questioning the validity of long-exhausted literary conventions and the ossified social and political structure of Syria. This led inevitably to his imprisonment and ultimately to his exile to Beirut, in 1956. Shortly afterwards, he became a naturalized Lebanese citizen.

In 1957, along with the Lebanese poet Yusuf al-Khal, he established the publishing house *Dar Majallat Shi'r*. In 1968 he founded the influential journal *Mawaqif*, the only widely circulated vehicle for experimental Arab poetry. In 1973 he was awarded a doctorate at the St Joseph University of Beirut.

In his poetry, critical writings, and anthologies, Adonis has always held that only a radical change in every aspect of Arab life would bring the Arabs into the twentieth century; only then would they be in a position to make a contribution to the advancement of humanity and of world civilization. He stressed that this could be achieved by exploring the Arab heritage and by exploiting its positive aspects and then linking these to the positive aspects of other civilizations.

The poetry and criticism of Adonis has had far-reaching influence on the development of Arab poetry. Indeed, he has created a new poetic language and rhythms, deeply rooted in classical poetry but employed to convey the predicament and responses of contemporary Arab society.

The Minaret

> A stranger arrived.
> The minaret wept:
> He bought it and topped it with a chimney.

Adonis revived and modified the classical form *qit'a* (short poem). He also developed and broadened the scope of the *qasida* (a pre-Islamic poetic form), and established the prose poem. It is no exaggeration to say that Adonis's role in Arab poetry has been similar in import to that of Pound and Eliot in British and American poetry.

مِرآةُ السيَّافِ

ـ هل قلتَ إنَّكَ شاعرٌ ؟

من أين جئتَ ؟ أُحِسُّ جلدكَ ناعماً ..
سيَّاف تسمعُني ؟
وهبتُكَ رأسَه ،
خذهُ ، وهاتِ الجلدَ واحذرْ أن يُمَسَّ
الجلدُ أشهى لي وأغلى ...

سيكون جلدك لي بساطاً
سيكون أجمل مخملٍ ،

هل قلت إنك شاعر ؟

A Mirror for the Executioner

"Did you say you're a poet?

Where do you come from? You have a fine skin.
Executioner, do you hear me?
You can have his head
    But bring me his skin unbruised.
    His skin means so much to me.
Take him away.

Your velvet skin
Will be my carpet.

Did you say you're a poet?"

مرآةٌ للقرن العشرينِ

تابوت يُلبَسُ وجْهَ الطفل
كتابْ
يُكْتَب في أحشاءِ غُرابْ
وحش يَتَقَدَّم ، يحمل زهرهْ

صَخْرَهْ
تتنفس في رئتيْ مجنونْ :

هوذا
هوذا القرن العشرونْ .

A Mirror for the Twentieth Century

A coffin bearing the face of a boy
A book
Written on the belly of a crow
A wild beast hidden in a flower

A rock
Breathing with the lungs of a lunatic:

This is it
This is the Twentieth Century.

مرآةٌ لبيروت
(١٩٦٧)

I

الشَّارع آمْرأَهْ
تقرأ ، حين تحزن ، الفاتحهْ
أو ترسم الصَّليبْ
والليل ، تحت نهدها ،
محـدَّب غريبْ

عبّأ في كيسه
كلابه الفضِّية النَّائِحَهْ
والأنجم المُطفأَهْ
والشَّارع آمْرَأَهْ
تَعُض كلَّ عابر
وآلجمل النَّائم حوْل صدرها
يغني
للنفطِ (كل عابر يغني)
والشَّارع اُمرأَهْ
تسقط في فراشها

A Mirror for Beirut
(1967)

I

The street is a woman who says
The *Fatiha* when she's grieved
Or makes the sign of the Cross.
Under her breast
The hunchbacked night
Fills his bag
With his grey whining dogs
And snuffed out stars.

The street is a woman who bites
The passersby.
The camel sleeping around her breast
Sings
For the oil shaikhs.
And the street is a woman who falls
On her bed.

II

ألوَرْد مرسوم على الأَحْذِيَهْ

والأرض والسَّماء
صندوق ألوان ـ

وفي الأَقْبِيَهْ
يرتسمُ التَّاريخُ كالتَّابوت

وفي أنين نجمة أو أمة تَموتْ
يضطجعُ الرِّجال والأطفالُ والنِّساءْ
بلَا سَرَاويل
ولا أغْطِيَهْ ...

III

جبانة ،
وصرة في الحِزامْ
من ذهب ،
وامرأة خشخاشة تنامْ
في حُضنها أمير أو خنجر
ينامْ .

II

Flowers painted on shoes.

The earth and sky trapped
in a box of colours.

In the cellars
History is carved like a coffin.

And in the cry of a star or a dying nation
Men, women and children sleep
Without trousers
Without blankets . . .

III

A cemetery.
A gold purse
tucked in a belt.
A babbling woman sleeps
With a prince or a dagger in her arms.

هـم
(حلم)

جاؤُوا
دخلوا البيت عراة
حفروا
طمروا الأطفال ، وعادوا ...

Worries
(A Dream)

They arrived naked
Broke into the house
Dug a hole
Buried the children and left . .

العصر الذهبي

ـ « جُرَّه يا شَرَطِيّ ... »
ـ « سيدي أعرف أن المِقْصَلْه
بانتظاري
غير أني شاعر أعبد ناري
وأحب الجُلجُله » .

ـ « جُرَّه يا شَرَطِيّ
قل له إن حذاء الشرَطيّ
هو من وجهك أجمل » .

آه يا عصر الحذاء الذهبي
أنت أغلى أنت أجمل .

The Golden Age

"Take him away, Officer . . . "
"Sir, I know the gallows
Are waiting for me
But I'm only a poet worshipping my fire
And I love Golgotha."

"Take him away, Officer!
Tell him: The Officer's boot
Is handsomer than your face."

Age of the golden boot
You are the handsomest and most expensive.

أغنيـة

ـ جاء في آخر اللَّيل في موسم الكهوُله
لم ينم في سرير الأساطير ،
لم يعرف الطفُوُله .

تنهض في جسدي أرض
تهمس لأيّامي أن تَكون شَبابيكُها ،
تعلم خطواتي أن تصير باسمها رسائل
وعصافيرْ ،

هكذا أعبُر كالزجاج ، شفّافاً ولا ظلّ لي ،
في طريق من الأجنحة ،
أتَحرَّر ، أَسجُن أعضَائِي داخِل أعضَائي
أصير كبَريق اللؤلؤة :
أضرُب العيون وأعود الى بُؤْرتي .

من يعطيني ورقة أُحَمِّلُهَا أكداساً من البخور والصَّندَل
أُنقّطهَا كالعَرُوس وأَجلُوها
أَقرأ عليها سورة مريم
أهزُّ فوقها جذوعي منَ الشَّوقِ والحلمِ
وأرْسِلُها إلى أحبَابي
مليئة كالتفَّاحَة
خفيفة وخَضراء كَمُهْرةِ الخضر !

Song

He came at the end of the night, at the season of old age.
He never slept in a bed of myths,
He didn't live his childhood.

The earth rises in my body
And tells my days to be its windows,
And teaches my steps its name so they can be its letters
And birds.

I go through a path of wings like glass,
Transparent and have no shadow,
Free myself, trap my limbs within my limbs,
And like the sparkle of a pearl
    I strike the eyes and return to my pupils.

Who will give me a piece of paper to wrap incense and sandalwood,
Adorn it with dots like a bride's make-up, polish it,
Bless it with the Koran's praise of the Madonna,
Shake my roots of longing and dreams over it
And send it to the loved ones,
Full like an apple,
Fine and green like Khadir's colt.

وأنتمْ ،

يا من تكرهون التَّلفُّظَ باسمي

تلصِقُوَني بعيونِكم حينَ تقرأون أخبارَ الوَفَيَات وتصرخون :

قسَماً ، يَسير وفي كُلِّ جَيْبة من جيوبه مِدفع وامرأة عارِية

أنتم أيُّها الملائكة

الأطْهارُ

الـمُنقِذُون

القُـوَّاد

الحُكَماء ... الخ ،

ألتمس منكم في هذِه اللَّحظة معْجِزة واحِدَة

أن تعرفوا كيف تقولُون : وَدَاعاً ، وَاوْ دَال أَلِف عَيْن أَلِف

معجزة واحدة : وداعاً

بيننا بُعد الرُّوح

بيننَا الأَعْماق والسَّفَر في فضَاء الأَعْماقِ .

You hate to say my name,
You always see me when you read obituaries
And scream:
    "I swear he has in his pockets a naked woman and a gun."

You angels,
    Pure ones,
        Liberators,
            Leaders,
                Wise men, etc . . .

At this moment all I ask of you is a miracle:
Just for you to know how to say Goodbye
GOODBYE
Just a miracle: a Goodbye

As distant as our souls
As distant as a journey into the space of the soul.

نُبُوءَةٌ

(حلم)

للوطن المحفُور في حياتنا كَالقبرْ
للوطن الـمُخَدَّر المقتولْ
تجيىء من سُبَاتِنَا الأَلْفِي ، مِن تَاريخنا المَشْلُولْ
شمس بِلاَ عِبادَهْ ،
تقتل شيخ الرَّمْلِ والجَرَادَهْ

والزمن النابت في سُهوبِهِ
اليابس في سُهوبِهِ
كالفِطرْ

شمس تحبُّ الفتك والإبادَهْ
تطلع من وراء هذا الجِسْرْ ...

Prophecy

From our thousand-year-old sleep,
From our crippled history
Comes a sun without ritual
To the country that's dug into our lives like a grave,
To the drugged and murdered country,
And kills the shaikh of the sand and locusts.

Time grows on its plains,
Time withers on its plains
Like mushrooms.

A sun that kills and destroys
Appears over the bridge.

مزمور

يقبل أعزل كالغابة وكَالغَيْم لايُرَدُّ ، وأمس حقل قارَّةً ونقل البحــر من مَكَانِهِ .

يرسم قفا النَّهارِ ، يصنع من قدميه نهاراً ويستعير حذاء اللَّيل ثم ينتظر ما لا يأتي .

حيثُ يصير الحجَرُ بحيرة والظِّلُّ مَدِينة ، يحيَا ـ يحيَا ويضلِّلُ اليَأَسَ ، مَاحِياً فَسحةَ الأَمَل ، راقصاً للتُراب كي يتثاءب ، وللشجر كَيْ يَنام .

وها هو يعلن تَقَاطع الأطراف ، ناقِشاً على جبينِ عصرنا علامة السّحر .

Psalm

He comes unarmed like a forest, like a destined cloud.
Yesterday he carried a continent and changed the
position of the sea.

He paints the back of day and creates daylight out of
his feet, borrows the night's shoes and waits for
what will not come.

He lives where the stone becomes a lake, the shadow a
city—he lives and fools despair, wiping out the
vastness of hope, dancing for the soil so it can yawn,
for the trees so they can sleep.

And here he is speaking of crossroads, drawing the
magic sign on the forehead of time.

يملأ الحياة ولا يراه أحد . يصيِّر الحياةَ زَبداً ويغوص فيه . يحول الغد إلى
طريدَة ويعدو يائساً وراءها . محفورة كلماته في اتجاه الضَّياع الضَّياع الضَّياع

والحيرةُ وطَنه ، لكنَّه مليء بالعُيون .

إنهُ الرِّيح لا ترجع القَهْقَرَى والماء لا يعودُ إلى منْبَعه . يخلق نوعه بدءاً من
نفسه ـ لا أسْلاَفَ له وفي خطَواته جُذُورُه .

يمشِي في الهاويةِ وله قامَةُ الرِّيح .

He fills life but no one sees him. He turns life into
foam and plunges into it. He turns tomorrow into a
prey and hopelessly pursues it. His words are
engraved in the direction of loss loss loss.

Doubt is his home, but he is full of eyes.

He is the wind that knows no retreat, the water that
does not return to its source. He creates his own
kind starting from himself—he has no ancestors and
his roots are in his footsteps.

He walks through the abyss in the form of the wind.

الجرح

I

أَلورق النائم تحتَ الريحْ
سفينة الجُرْحْ
والزمنُ الهَالِك مَجْد الجُرُحْ
والشَّجَر الطَّالِع في أهْدابِنا
بحيْرَة لِلْجُرْحْ .

والجُرْح في الجسُورْ
حِينَ يَطُول القَبْرْ
حين يطولُ الصَّبْرْ
بينَ حَوافي حُبِّنا ومَوْتِنا ، والجُرْحْ
إيَماءةٌ ، والجُرْح في العُبورْ .

II

للغة المخنوقة الأَجراسْ
أمنح صوتَ الجُرْحْ

The Wound

I

The leaves sleeping under the winds
Are boats for the wound.
The buried past is the glory of the wound.
The trees growing in your eyelashes
Are lakes for the wound.

The wound is in the crosspoint
When the grave reaches
When patience reaches
The tips of our love, our death.
The wound is a sign
The wound is in the crossing.

II

I give the voice of the wound
To a speech with choked bells.
I light the fire of the wound.

للحجَر المُقبِل من بَعيدْ
للعالَم اليابِسِ لِلبَيَاسْ
للزَّمن المحْمُول في نقَالة الجليدْ
أشعلُ نارَ الجُرْح ؛

وحينَما يحترق التاريخ في ثيابي
وتنبت الأظافِر الزرقاء في كِتابي
وحينما أصيح بالنَّهارْ ـ
من أنت ، من يرميك في دفاتِري
في أرْضِيَ البَتولْ ؟
ألمحُ في دَفاتري في أرضي البَتُول
عيْنين مِنْ غُبَارْ
أسمعُ من يَقول :
« أنا هو الجُرح الذِّي يَصيرْ
يكبرُ في تاريخكَ الصغيرْ » .

III

سَمَّيْتُكَ السَّحاب
يا جُرْح يا يمامةَ الرحيلْ
سَمَّيْتُكَ الرِّيشَةَ والكِتَابْ
وها أنا أبْتَدِىءُ الحِوَارْ
بيني وبين اللغة العريقة

For a stone coming from far away,
For a dried up world, for drought,
For time carried on a stretcher of ice.

When history burns in my clothes
And blue nails grow in my book,
When I shout at daylight
"Who are you, who's thrown you on my books,
On my virgin land?"
I see in my books, in my virgin land
Eyes of dust.
I hear someone saying:
"I am the flourishing wound
Of your small history."

III

I have called you a cloud,
Wound, turtle-dove of departure.
I have called you a feather and a book.
And here I am starting conversation
With a noble word

في جزرِ الأسفارْ
في أرْخَبيل السقطة العَريقهْ
وهَا أناَ أعلِّمُ الحوارْ
للرِّيح والنَّخِيل
يا جُرح يا يمامة الرَّحيلْ .

IV

لو كانَ لي في وطَنِ الأحلامِ والمرَأَيا
مَرافئٌ ، لو كان لي سِفينَهْ
لو أن لي بَقايا
مدينَة لو أنَّ لي مَدينهْ
في وطن الأطفال والبُكاءْ ،

لصُغت هذا كلَّه للجُرْحْ
أغنية كالرُّمحْ
تختَرق الأشجَار والحجَار والسَّماءْ
لَيِّنَةً كالماءْ
جامِحَة مَذْهُولةً كالفتحْ .

V

أمْطِر على صَحرائنا
يا عَالماً مزَيَّناً بالحلمْ والحَنين

In the shifting of islands,
In the archipelago of the noble fall.
And here I am teaching conversation
To the wind and palm trees,
Wound, turtle-dove of departure.

IV

If I had havens in a country of mirrors and dreams,
If I had a ship,
If I had the remains of a city,
Or a city
In a country of children and weeping

I'd have made out of all this for the wound
A song like a spear
Piercing trees, stones and heaven,
And soft as water,
Overpowering and amazing like a conquest.

V

Rain on our deserts,
World charged with a dream and longing.

أمطِرْ ، ولكن هُزَّنا ، نحنُ ، نَخِيلَ الجُرْحْ
واكسِر لنا غُصْنَيْنْ
مِنْ شجر يَعْشَقُ صمْت الجُرْح
من شجر يَسْهَرُ فوق الجرح
مُقَوَّس الأهْدَابِ واليَدَيْن .

يا عالَماً مُزَيَّناً بالحُلم والحَنِين
يا عالَماً يَسْقُطُ في جَبيني
مُرْتَبِساً كالجُرح
لا تَقتَرب ، أقرَب مِنْك الجُرح
لا تغرِني ، أجْمَل منك الجُرحْ
وذلك السِّحْر الذي رَمَته
عَيْناك في المَمَالِك الأخِيرَه
مَرَّ عَلَيْه الجُرْحْ
مَرَّ فلمْ يَتْرُك لَهُ شراعاً
يغوي ، ولم يتْرُكْ لَهُ جَزِيرَه .

Rain and shake us, we the palm trees of the wound,
And snap two branches for us
From the trees that love the silence of the wound,
From the trees that stay awake over the wound
With arched eyelashes and hands.

World charged with a dream and longing,
World falling on my forehead
And drawn like a wound,
Don't come closer, the wound is nearer than you,
Don't tempt me, the wound is more beautiful than you.
The wound is beyond the fate
Your eyes cast
On the lost civilizations.
It's left no sails
Nor islands.

امرأة ورجل
(حوار ، سنة ١٩٦٧)

ـ من أنتَ ؟

ـ بهلول بلا مَكَانْ

من حجر الفَضاء من سلَالة الشَّيطانْ

ـ من أنتِ ؟

هل سافَرتِ في جسدي ؟

ـ مراراً ؟

ـ ما رأيتِ ؟

ـ رأيتُ موتي

ـ هَرَوَلتِ فوق دَمي ، جلستِ ، نزعْتِ ثوبك ، واغتسلتِ ، لبستِ وجهي ؟

ورأيتِ شمسي مثل ظلٍّ

ورأيتِ ظلي مثل شمسٍ

ونزلت تحت سَريرتي ، وكَشفْتِني ؟

ـ أكَشفْتَني ؟

ـ كَاشَفْتِني ؟ أيقنْتِ ؟

ـ لا

ـ أشفيتِ بي ، وبقيتِ خائفة ؟

ـ بلى

ـ أَعَرَفْتِني ؟

ـ أَعَرَفْتِني ؟

A Woman and a Man
(Conversation, 1967)

WOMAN: Who are you?

MAN: A clown without a home,
A meteorite, a son of Satan.
Who are you?
Have you travelled in my body?

WOMAN: Many times.

MAN: What did you see?

WOMAN: My death.

MAN: Have you crept in my blood, sat down,
Undressed, washed and worn my face?
Seen my sun like a shadow
My shadow like the sun
And explored my soul?

WOMAN: Do you know me now?

MAN: Have you told me all? Are you sure?

WOMAN: No.

MAN: You got what you want from me? Still afraid?

WOMAN: Yes.

MAN: Do you know me now?

WOMAN: Do you know me now?

نوح الجديد

I

رحنا مع الفلكِ ، مجاديفنا
وعد من الله وتحت المطرْ
والوحْل ، نَحيا ويموت البشرْ .
رُحْنَا مَعَ المَوْج وكان الفَضَاء
حبْلا من الموتى ربَطْنا به
أعْمَارنا وكان بَيْنَ السَّمَاء
وَبيْنَنَا نافِذَة للدُّعاءْ :

« يَا رَبُّ ، لِمَ خَلَّصْتنا وحْدنا
من بين كل الناسِ والكائناتْ ؟
وأين تلْقِيناً ، أفِي أرْضِك الأُخْرَى ،
أفِي موْطِننا الأَوَّلِ
في ورق المَوْت وريح الحيَاة ؟
يا ربُّ فينا ، في شرَايينَنا
رُعْب من الشَّمْسِ ؛ يَئْسنا من النُور
يئِسنا من غَدٍ مُقْبِلٍ
فيه نعيد العمر من أوَّلِ .

The New Noah

I

We sailed in the Ark
Our oars were God's promises.
Under the rain and dirt
We survived, but not mankind.
We went along with the waves
And the sky was like a rope of dead people
On which we tied our lives.
Through a window of prayers we reached the sky.

"Lord, why did you save us above all other
People and creatures?
Where will you throw us, to your other land,
To our original home,
To the leaves of death, to the wind of life?
Lord, our fear of the sun
Runs in our blood. We have lost faith in light,
We have lost faith in tomorrow
Where we used to begin a new life.

« آه ، لو أنَّا لم نصر بذْرَة
للخلق ، للأرضِ وأجيَاها
آه ـ لو أنَّا لمْ نزلْ طِينة
أو جْمرَة ، أو لم نَزُلْ بين بين
كيْ لا نَرَى العالم كي لا نرى
جحيمه وربَّهُ مرَّتين . »

II

لو رَجَعَ الزَّمان من أول
وغمرت وجه الحياة الميَاه
وارتَجَّت الأرض وخَفَّ الإله
ـ يقول لي يَانوح أنْقِذْ لنا
الأَحْيَاءَ ـ لم أحْفَلْ بقولِ الإله
ورحتُ في فُلْكي ،
أزيحُ الحَصَى والطِّين عَن مَحَاجرِ الميِّتين
أفتحُ للطُوْفانِ أعماقهمَ ،
أهمس في عروقِهم أننَا

Oh, if only we had not been a seed
Of creation, of the earth,
If only we had remained soil or live coals,
If only we had stayed half-way
So as not to see the world,
So as not to see its hell and its God twice."

II

If time was to start all over again
And life's face was covered with water
And the earth trembled and God was mad
And Noah asked me: "Save the living"
I would not listen to God,
I would go about on my Ark
Clearing the pebbles and dirt
From the sockets of the dead,
Opening their souls to the flood,
Whispering in their veins:

عدْنا من التِّيهِ ، خرَجْنا من الكهف
وغيرنا سماءَ السِّنين ،
وأننا نبحر لا ننثَني رعباً
ولا نصغِي لقولِ الإله

موعدنا موت
وشطآننا يأس ألِفْنَاه ، رضينا به
بحراً جليدياً حديد المياه
نعبرُه نمضي إلى مُنتَهاه ،
نمضي ولا نصُغي لذاكَ الإله
تُقنا إلى رَبٍّ جديد سِواه .

We have returned from our wanderings,
We have come out of the cave
And changed the sky of years,
We are sailing and fear cannot bend us,
And we do not listen to God's word.

We have an appointment with death,
We have become familiar with our shores of despair,
We have grown to accept its frozen sea with iron water,
And we sail through it to its end.
We carry on moving and never listen to that God,
We long for a new god.

الأيام السبعة

أيها الأم التي تسخر
من حبي ومقتي ،
أنتِ في سبعة أيام خلقت
فَخَلقْتِ الموج والافق
وريش الأغنيهْ ،

وأنا أيامي السبعة جرح وغرابُ
فلماذا الأحجيهْ
وأنا مثلك ريح وترابُ ؟

The Seven Days

Mother, do not mock
My love, my hate.
You were created in seven days
And you created the waves, the horizon,
The plume of the song.

My seven days are a wound and a crow
So why all these riddles
Since I'm like you, wind and earth.

اللؤلؤة

(الحلم ـ المرآة)

كيف أمشي نحو شعبي ، نحو نفسي

كيف أمضي نحو تَهْيَامي وصوتي ، كيف أصعدْ ؟

لست إلا نهراً يرفض ، يخبو ، يتوقدْ

غامراً لؤلؤة الشِّعر الخَفِيَّه

لابساً وسوسة الشمس ،

وإلا

حلماً

أنِّيَ حُمَّى نبويَّة

أنني ضوء يَلفَّ الليل ، يَعْرى

سائحاً في جسد الليل ،

وأنِّي

جامحٌ

أحتضن الأرض كأنثىَ

وأنامُ

قارِعاً ناقوسيَ البحريَّ فيها

لهباً يفتح ،

يستنزل فيها

آيَةً ،

أنِّي كتابٌ

ودمي حبرٌ

وأعضائي كلامٌ .

The Pearl
(Dream – Mirror)

How can I walk towards my people, towards myself?
How can I walk towards my passion, my voice? How can I ascend?
I am only a river that rejects, surges, blazes;
     Overwhelming poetry's hidden pearl,
     Wearing the sun's suspicion;
Or
A dream.
     I am the fever of prophethood.
     I am the light that enfolds the dark,
     Naked, wandering in the night's body.
     Obsessed
     I
     Hold the earth like a woman
          And sleep,
Ringing my sea-bell
          To spread a flame,
          To summon a sign.
          I am a book
          My blood is ink
          And my limbs are words.

كيف أمشي نحو نفسي ، نحو شعبي
ودمي نار وتاريخي رُكام ؟
أَسْنِدُوا صَدْري ـ
في صدري حريقٌ
ومزامير ،
جبالٌ وكُرومُ
ومسافات
وأجساد عُصورٍ تتَجرجر
ونجوم
والتَّواريخ مرايا
والحضارات مرايا
تَتَكَسَّر .

لا ، دعوني :
إنني أَسْمَع أصواتا تُغَنِّي في رمادي
إنني ألمحها تمشِي كأطفال بلادي .

How can I walk towards myself, towards my people,
When my blood is fire, my history a heap of ruins?
Give support to my chest—
   There is a fire in my breast,
     Psalms,
  Mountains, vines,
     Distances,
  Bodies dragged from all periods,
Stars.
And histories are mirrors
And civilizations are mirrors
Smashed to pieces.

No, leave me alone:
I hear voices singing in my ashes,
I see them walking like the children of my country.

المئذنة

بكت المئذنهْ
حين جاء الغريبُ ـ اشتراها
وبنى فَوقَهَا مدخَنهْ .

The Minaret

A stranger arrived.
The minaret wept:
He bought it and topped it with a chimney.

الصحراء
(مختارات من يوميات حصار بيروت ١٩٨٢)

‑ ١ ‑

... في زمانٍ
يُصارحني : لستَ مني
وأصارحهُ : لستُ منك ، وأجهَدُ أن أفهَمَه
وأنا الآن طيفٌ
يتشرَّد في غابةٍ
داخل الجُمْجِمَه .

‑ ٢ ‑

واقفٌ ، والجدارُ سياجٌ ‑
مدًى يتضاءلُ ، نافذة تَتَناءَى

والنَّهار خيوط
تتقطعُ في رئتَيَّ وترفُو المساءَ .

The Desert
(The Diary of Beirut Under Siege, 1982)

1

My era tells me bluntly:
You do not belong.
I answer bluntly:
I do not belong,
I try to understand you.
Now I am a shadow
Lost in the forest
Of a skull.

2

I'm on my feet, the wall is a fence—
    The distance shrinks, a window recedes.
Daylight is a thread
Snipped by my lungs to stitch the evening.

- ٣ -

صخرة تحت رأسي ، -
كل ما قلتهُ عن حَياتي وعن موتها
يتكرّرُ في صَمتها ...

- ٤ -

أتناقَض ؟ هذا صَحيح
فأنا الآن زرع وبالأمس كنتُ حصاداً
وأنا بين ماءٍ ونارٍ
وأنا الآن جَمرٌ وورد
وأنا الآن شمسٌ وظلٌ
وأنا لستُ ربّا -
أتناقض ؟ هذا صحيحٌ ...

- ٥ -

دائماً يلبَس القمرْ
ليقاتِل أشباحَهُ ،
خوذةً من حجرْ .

3

All I said about my life and death
Recurs in the silence
Of the stone under my head . . .

4

Am I full of contradictions? That is correct.
    Now I am a plant. Yesterday, when I was between fire
      and water
    I was a harvest.
    Now I am a rose and live coal,
    Now I am the sun and the shadow
    I am not a god.
Am I full of contradictions? That is correct . . .

5

The moon always wears
A stone helmet
To fight its own shadows.

‐ ٦ ‐

مغلق باب بيتي
والظَّلامُ لحافٌ :
قمر شاحِب ، حامِل في يديهْ
حفنة من ضِياء ،
عجزت كلماتي
أنْ توجِّهَ شُكري إليهْ .

‐ ٧ ‐

غَيَّرَ القتْل شكْل المدينة ، ‐ هذا الحجرْ
من عظام ،
وهذا الدخان زَفيرُ البشرْ .

‐ ٨ ‐

لم نعدْ نَتَلاقى
لم يعد بيننا غيرُ نبْذٍ ونفْيٍ
والمواعيدُ ماتَتْ ، ومات الفَضاءْ ،
وحدَه الموت صارَ اللقاءْ .

6

The door of my house is closed.
    Darkness is a blanket:
        A pale moon comes with
        A handful of light
        My words fail
        To convey my gratitude.

7

The killing has changed the city's shape—This rock
        Is bone
        This smoke people breathing.

8

We no longer meet,
Rejection and exile keep us apart.
The promises are dead, space is dead,
Death alone has become our meeting point.

- ٩ -

أغلق الباب ، لا لِيُقيِّد أفراحَهُ ،
... ليحرِّر أحزانَهُ .

- ١٠ -

إعلان -
عَن عاشقةٍ
قُتِلتْ ،
عن طفل مخطوف ،
والشرطي جِدارٌ .

- ١١ -

كل شيء سيأتي قديم ،
فاصطَحبْ غير هذا الجنون - تَهيَّأْ
كي تَظَلَّ غريباً ...

9

He shuts the door
Not to trap his joy
. . . But to free his grief.

10

A newscast
　　About a woman in love
　　Being killed,
　　About a boy being kidnapped
　　And a policeman growing into a wall.

11

Whatever comes it will be old
　　So take with you anything other than this madness—get ready
　　　　To stay a stranger . . .

142

‑ ١٢ ‑

ـ وجدوا أشخاصاً في أكيَاسٍ :
شخص لا رأسَ لَهُ
شخص دون يديْنٍ ودون لِسانٍ
شخص مَفْروم
والباقون بلا أسماءْ .
ـ أجُننتَ ؟ رجاءً
لا تكتبْ عن هذي الأشياءْ .

‑ ١٣ ‑

سوف ترى
قل اسمهُ
أو قل رَسمْتُ وجههُ
مُدَّ يديك نحوهُ
أو سِرْ كما يسير كل راجلٍ
أو ابتسمْ
أو قُلْ حزنت مرةً .
سَوفَ تَرَى
ليس هناكَ وطنٌ ...

12

They found people in sacks:
    One without a head
    One without a tongue or hands
    One squashed
    The rest without names.
Have you gone mad? Please,
    Do not write about these things.

13

You will see
    Say his name
    Say I painted his face
    Stretch your hand to him
    Or walk like any man
    Or smile
    Or say I was once sad
You will see
    There is no homeland . . .

- ١٤ -

ربما جاء وقت ستقبل فيهِ
أن تعيش أَصَمَّ وأبكَمَ ، لكنْ
ربما سمحوا أن تُتَمتِمَ : موتٌ ،
وحياة ، وبعثٌ -
والسلام عليكم .

- ١٥ -

يتزيَّا بزَي الجهاد ، ويَرْفُلُ في بَزةٍ من فِكَر
تاجر - لا يبيع الثيابَ ، يبيع البَشَرْ .

- ١٦ -

أخذوه الى حُفْرةٍ ، حرقوهُ
لم يكن قاتلا ، كان طفلًا
لم يكنْ ...
كان صوتاً
يتموَّج ، يرقى على درجات الفضاءْ ،
وهو ، الآن ، شَبَّابَةٌ في الهواءْ .

14

There may come a time when you'll be
    Accepted to live deaf and dumb, and perhaps
They'll let you mumble: death,
        Life, resurrection—
    And peace be upon you.

15

He wears Jihad uniform, struts in a mantle of ideas.
A merchant—he does not sell clothes, he sells people.

16

They took him to a ditch and burnt him.
    He was not a murderer, he was a boy.
    He was not . . .
                He was a voice
Vibrating, scaling the steps of space.
And now he's fluting in the air.

‑ ١٧ ‑

ظلماتٌ ‑
شجر الأرضِ دمعٌ على وَجَناتِ السماءْ
والمكان انْخِسَافٌ ، ‑
كسرَ الموتُ غصنَ المدينةِ وارتحل الأصدقاءْ .

‑ ١٨ ‑

لا تموت لأنك مِن خَالقٍ ، أو لأنَّك هذا الجسدْ
أنت ميتٌ لأنَّكَ وجْهُ الأَبدْ .

‑ ١٩ ‑

زهرة أغوتِ الرِّيح كي تنقُل الرائِحه ،
ماتتِ البارِحَهْ .

‑ ٢٠ ‑

لم تَعُد تشرق الشمسُ ، ‑ تَنْسَلُّ في خفيةٍ
وتُوَاري
قدميْها بقشٍ ...

17

Darkness.
The earth's trees have become tears on heaven's cheeks.
An eclipse in this place.
Death snapped the city's branch and the friends departed.

18

You do not die because you are created or because you have a body
    You die because you are the face of the future.

19

The flower that tempted the wind to carry its perfume
                                        Died yesterday.

20

The sun no longer rises
It covers its feet with straw
And slips away . . .

ـ ٢١ ـ

أتوقَّع أن يأتي الموتُ ، ليلًا ، ـ
أن يوسِّد أحضانَهُ
وردةً ـ
تعبت من غبارٍ يُغطي جبينَ السَّحَرْ
تعبت من زفيرِ البشرْ .

ـ ٢٢ ـ

من نبيذ النخيل إلى هدأةِ الصحارى ... إلى آخرِهْ
من صباح يُهرِّبُ أحشاءَهُ
وينام على كتف التائهين ... إلخ ،(*)
من شوارع ، من شاحناتٍ
للجنود ، الحُشُود ... إلخ ،
من ظلالِ رجالٍ نساءٍ ... إلخ ،
من قنابلَ مَحْشوَّةٍ
بدماء الحنيفينَ والكافرينَ ... إلخ ،
من حَديدٍ يَنزُّ صَديداً وينزف لحماً ... إلخ ،
من حقولٍ تَحِنُّ إلى القمح
والعشب والعاملين ... إلخ ،
من قلاعٍ تُسَوِّرُ أجسادنا
وتهيل علينا الظلامَ ... إلخ ،

(* تقرأ بلفظها الكامل ، كما هي واردة في السطر الأول .)

21

I expect death to come at night
  To cushion his lap with
          A rose—
I'm tired of the dust covering the forehead of dawn
I'm tired of the breathing of people.

22

From the palm wine to the calmness of the desert . . . etc.
From a morning that smuggles its stomach
  And sleeps on the shoulders of the refugees . . . etc.
From the streets, army vehicles,
  Concentration of troops . . . etc.
From the shadows of men, women . . . etc.
From bombs stuffed with the blood of Muslims
  and infidels . . . etc.
From the flesh of iron that bleeds
  and sweats pus . . . etc.
From the fields that long for the wheat, the green and the
  workers . . . etc.
From castles walling our bodies
  And bombarding us with darkness . . . etc.

من خرافات موتى ، تقول الحياةَ ـ تقود الحياةَ ... إلخ ،
من كلام هو الذَّبح ، والذَّبح ، والذَّابحون ... إلخ ،
من ظلام ظلام ظلام
أتنفس ، أَلْمس جسميَ ـ أبحث عنِّي
وعنك ، وعنه ، وعن غيرنا .
وَأعلّق موتي
بين وجهي وهذا الكلام ـ النَّزيفِ ... إلخ .

ـ ٢٣ ـ

شجرٌ ينحني ليقولَ وداعاً
زهرٌ يتفتَّح ، يَزْهو ، يُنكّس أوراقه ليقولَ وداعاً
طرق كالفواصل بين التنفسِ والكلماتِ تقول وداعاً
جسدٌ يلبس الرمل ، يسقط في تيههِ ليقول وداعاً
ورقٌ يعشقُ الحبرَ
والأبجديةَ والشعراءَ يقول وداعاً
والقصيدة قالت وداعاً .

ـ ٢٤ ـ

قاتلٌ
في هواء المدينة

From the myths of the dead which speak of
  life—express life . . . etc.
From the speech which is the slaughter, the slaughtered
  and the slaughterers . . . etc.
From the dark dark dark
I breathe, feel my body—search for you and him,
  myself and others.

I hung my death
Between my face and these bleeding words . . . etc.

23

Trees bow to say goodbye
Flowers open, glow, lower their leaves to say goodbye,
Roads like pauses between the breathing and the words say goodbye,
A body wears hope, falls in a wilderness to say goodbye,
The papers that love ink,
            The alphabet, the poets say goodbye,
And the poem says goodbye.

24

The killer
In the air

يسبح في جرْحِها ، -
جرحها سقطةٌ
زلزلت باسمها
بنزيفِ اسمِها
كل ما حولَنا
أَلبيوتُ تغادر جدرانَها
وأنا لاأنا .

صفحةٌ من كتابٍ
تتمرأى قنابلُ فيها
تتمرأى النُّبوات والحكمُ الغابرَهْ
تتمرأى محاريبُ / سجادةٌ من حروفٍ
تتساقطُ خيطاً فخيطاً
فوق وجه المدينةِ من إبَر الذاكره .

غرقت نجمةٌ في الدِّماءْ -
أَلدماءِ التي كان طفلٌ يحدّث عنها
ويوشوش أصحابَهُ :

Swims in the city's wound—
      The wound is the fall
      That shakes with its name
      With its bleeding name
Everything around us.
The houses leave their walls
And I am
Not I

25

In a page of a book
Bombs see themselves,
Prophetic sayings and ancient wisdom see themselves,
Niches see themselves.
The threads of carpet words
Go through memory's needle
Over the city's face.

26

A star was drowned in blood,
The blood a boy was talking about
And whispering to his friends:

لم يعد في السماءْ
غيرُ بعض الثقوب التي سُمِّيت أنجماً ...

‑ ٢٧ ‑

أللّيلُ نهارٌ يولدُ ليلًا
في هذي الدَّرْبْ
ضوءُ الشَّمس وضوءُ الشمع سواءٌ
في ظلماتِ القلبْ .

‑ ٢٨ ‑

خطأٌ أقنع الشمس ألا تقولْ
ما الذي دونته الحقولُ ولم تَرْوه الفصولْ .

Only some holes known as stars
Remain in the sky.

27

The night is daylight born black
    On this path.
Sunlight and candlelight are the same
    In the heart's darkness.

28

It's wrong
To convince the sun not to say
What's been written by the fields but not told by the seasons.

يَهبطُ الليلُ [هذا

ورق كان أعطاه للحِبْر ـ [حبر الصباح الذي لم يجيء]

يهبط الليل فوق السريرِ ـ [السريرِ الذي كان هيَّأه عاشقٌ لم يجيءْ]

يهبط الليلُ / لا صوتَ [غيمٌ . دخانٌ]

يهبط الليل [شخص ـ في يديه أرانبُ ؟ نملٌ ؟]

يهبط الليلُ [سور البناية يهتز . كل الستائر شفَّافةٌ]

يهبط الليل ، يصغي : [نجوم كما يعرف الليل خرساءُ ، والشجرات الأخيرةُ

في آخر السورِ لا تتذكر شيئاً

من كلام الهواءِ لأغْصَانِهَا]

يهبط الليل [بين النوافذِ والريح همسٌ]

يهبط الليلُ [ضوء تسربَ . جارٌ يتمدد في عُريهِ]

يهبط الليلُ [شخصان . ثوب يعانق ثوباً ـ والنوافذ شفافةٌ]

يهبط الليلُ [هذا مزاجٌ : قمرُ الليل يشكو لسروالهِ

ما شكاه المحبُّون دوماً]

يهبط الليل [يرتاح في جَرةٍ

مُلئت خمرة . لا نِدامَى .

رجلٌ واحدٌ يتقلَّبُ في كأسهِ]

29

The night descends (these are the papers he gave to the ink—
    morning's ink that never came)
The night descends on the bed (the bed of the
    lover who never came)
The night descends/not a sound (clouds. Smoke)
The night descends (someone had in his hands rabbits? Ants?)
The night descends (the wall of the building shakes. All the
    curtains are transparent)
The night descends, listens (the stars as the night knows are
    dumb,
    and the last trees at the end of the
    wall remember nothing of what the air
    said to their branches)
The night descends (the wind whispers to the windows)
The night descends (the light penetrates. A neighbour lies
    in his nakedness)
The night descends (two people. A dress holding a dress—
    and the windows are transparent)
The night descends (this is a whim: the moon complains to his
    trousers
    about what the lovers have always complained of)
The night descends (he relaxes in a pitcher
    filled with wine. No friends
    just one man turning in his glass)

يهبط الليل [يحملُ بعضَ العناكبِ ، يرتاحُ للحشراتِ التي لا تسيء لغـير البيوتِ . إشارات ضوءٍ : ملاك أتى ، أم قذائفُ ، أم دعوةٌ ؟ وجاراتُنا كلهن ذهبنَ إلى الحج/ عُدْنَ أقلَّ ضموراً وأكثرَ غنجاً]

يهبط الليل [يدخلُ بين ثديِّ الأيامى/ وجاراتنا أيامى]

يهبط الليلُ [تلكَ ، الأريكةُ / تلك ، الوسادةُ : هذي ممرُّ ، وهذي مقرُّ]

يهبط الليل [ماذا نُعِدُّ ؟ نبيذاً ؟ أم ثريداً وخبـزاً ؟ يخبىء الليل عنـا شَهَيَّةَ أحشائهِ]

يهبط الليل [يلهو قليلاً

مع حـلازينِهِ ؛ مع حمامٍ غريبٍ ونجهلُ من أين جاءَ ، ومع حشراتٍ لم ترد في فصولِ الكتاب الذي خطه اللقاحُ عن الحيوانِ وأجناسه]

يهبط الليلُ [رعدٌ ـ أم ضجيجُ الملائكِ جاءَتْ بأفراسِها ؟]

يهبط الليل [يهذي

يتقلَّبُ في كأسِهِ ...]

The night descends (carries a few spiders, feels at ease with
insects which are a pest only to houses/
signs of light: an angel coming, missiles
or an invitation? Our women neighbours have
gone on pilgrimage/come back less slim
and more coquettish)
The night descends (enters between the breasts of the days/
our women neighbours are my days).
The night descends (that sofa/that pillow: this is an alleyway,
this is a place).
The night descends (what shall we prepare? Wine? Soup and bread?
The night hides from us his stomach's appetite).
The night descends (plays for a short while with his snails, with
strange doves which came from an unknown land,
and with the insects not mentioned in the
chapters of the book about reproduction among
different animal species)
The night descends (thunder—or is it the noise of angels coming
on their horses?)
The night descends (mumbling
turning in his glass . . .)

_ ٣٠ _

ـ حينما تفتح الشمس مخدَعها للمساءْ
تتراءى النوارس منسوجةً غطاءً
فوق وجه السماءْ .

_ ٣١ _

كتب القصيدةَ (لست أعرفُ أين تبتدىء الطريقُ ـ
وكيف أُسلم جبهتي لشعاعها ؟)
كتَب القصيدةَ (كيف أقنعه بأن غدي صحارَى
ودمي سرابُ رِمَالِهَا ؟)
كتَب القصيدةَ (من يزحزحُ صخرة الكلماتِ عنّي ؟)
كتب القصيدةَ (لست مِنَا
إن أنتَ لم تقتل أخاً ...)
كتب القصيدةَ (سوف يحدث غير ما يتوقَّعُونَ ،
ومَا يخالف كل ظنٍ ...)
كتَب القصيدةَ (كيف نفهمُ هذه اللغة الطَّريده
بين الحقيقةِ والقصيده ؟)
كتَب القصيدةَ (هل سيقدرُ ذلك القمر المشرد أن يعانقَ شمسَهُ ؟)
كتَب القصيدةَ (بين وجه الشمس والأفقِ التباسُ)
كتَب القصيدةَ (... / فَلْيَمُتْ ...

30

When the sun opens her bedroom for the evening
The seagulls appear as a cloth
Covering the face of the sky.

31

He wrote in a poem (I don't know where the road begins—
and how to surrender my forehead to its rays)
He wrote in a poem (how can I convince him my future is a desert
and my blood its mirage of sand?)
He wrote in a poem (who will shake the hardness of words off me?)
He wrote in a poem (you don't belong
if you don't kill a brother ...)
He wrote in a poem (what's going to happen is not what they expect
and contrary to what's been thought ...)
He wrote in a poem (how can we understand this fugitive language
caught between the truth and the poem?)
He wrote in a poem (can the refugee moon embrace its candle?)
He wrote in a poem (there's confusion
between the sun's face and the sky)
He wrote in a poem (... /let him die ...

- ٣٢ -

المدائنُ تنحلُّ ،
والأرض قاطرةٌ من هَبَاءْ :
وحده ، الحبُّ
يعرفُ أن يتزوجَ هذا الفضاءْ .

- ٣٣ -

مات . أرثيهِ ؟ لكن
ما أقولُ ؟ أقولُ : « حياتكَ لفظٌ ومَوْتُكَ معنىً ؟ »
أم أقولُ : « الطريق إلى الضوء تبدأ من غابة الظّلماتِ ؟ »

لغطٌ ... إنَّهْم ... /
تخبّأتُ في غارٍ وأغلقتُ بابهُ بصلاتي .

32

The cities break up
The earth is a train of dust
Only love
Knows how to marry this space.

33

He is dead. Should I mourn him?
What should I say? Should I say: your life was a word, your
  death its meaning?
Or should I say: the road to the light begins in the forest of
  darkness?

Confusion . . . They are . . .
  I hide myself in a cave and close the doors with prayers.

ـ ٣٤ ـ

تركَ القافلهْ
ومزاميرَها وهواها /
مفردٌ ، ذابلٌ
جذبته إلى عِطرها
وردةٌ ذابِلهْ .

ـ ٣٥ ـ

ستظلُّ صديقي
بين ما كان ، أو ما تبقّى
بين هذا الحطامْ
أيهذا البريقُ الذي يَلْبَسُ الغيمَ ، يا سّيداً لا ينامْ .

(٤ حزيران ١٩٨٢ ـ أول كانون الثاني ١٩٨٣)

34

He left the caravan train,
   Ignored its flute and its temptations.
Withering alone
   Drawn by a withering rose
   To its scent.

35

You will remain my friend
Of what was or what's left
   In this rubble
Oh, light that wears the clouds, the Lord that never sleeps.

(4 June 1982 – 1 January 1983)

سميح القاسم

أدونيس

المحتـــويات

محمود درويش